D0876675

Shaykh Fadhlalla Haeri is a writer-philosopher who combines knowledge and experience of the spiritual teachings of the East with a keen understanding of the West. He was raised in a family of several generations of well-known spiritual leaders in the Holy City of Kerbala, in Iraq. Shaykh Fadhlalla was educated in Europe and America in the field of science and technology. His professional experience was primarily as a consultant in industry and business, before embarking upon extensive travelling and teaching.

Shaykh Fadhlalla's re-discovery of the true Islamic heritage enables him to understand and relate to the spiritual quest wherever it may arise, irrespective of cultural or ethnic backdrops. His books and writings make original Islam available to the Western reader with an emphasis on its gnostic teachings.

Barnes + Noble
(Maplegrove)
January 12, 1997

The *Elements Of* is a series designed to present high quality introductions to a broad range of essential subjects.

The books are commissioned specifically from experts in their fields. They provide readable and often unique views of the various topics covered, and are therefore of interest both to those who have some knowledge of the subject, as well as those who are approaching it for the first time.

Many of these concise yet comprehensive books have practical suggestions and exercises which allow personal experience as well as theoretical understanding, and offer a valuable source of information on many important themes.

THE ELEMENTS OF
SUFISM

Shaykh Fadhlalla Haeri

ELEMENT

Shaftesbury, Dorset ● Rockport, Massachusetts
Brisbane, Queensland

© Shaykh Fadhlalla Haeri 1990

First published in Great Britain in 1990 by
Element Books Limited
Shaftesbury, Dorset SP7 8BP

Published in the USA in 1993 by
Element Books, Inc.
PO Box 830, Rockport, MA 01966

Published in Australia in 1993 by
Element Books Limited for
Jacaranda Wiley Limited,
33 Park Road, Milton, Brisbane 4064

Reprinted 1993
Reprinted 1994
Reprinted 1995

Cover illustration by Jeremy Norton
Cover design by Max Fairbrother
Typeset by Selectmove, London
Printed and bound in Great Britain by
Biddles Limited, Guildford and King's Lynn

British Library Cataloguing in Publication Data
Haeri, Fadhlalla
The elements of Sufism.
1. Sufism.
I. Title
297.4

Library of Congress Cataloging in Publication
data available

ISBN 1–85230–159–7

CONTENTS

ACKNOWLEDGEMENTS

This book has come about as a result of a direct question and request from Michael Mann as to the reality of Sufism. He knows that I am not an academic, nor am I interested in debate or controversy. He also knows that whatever I say will come from my heart and is based on experience. I thank him for his trust, persistence and patience.

Dr Latimah Peerwani nursed this book all along, and verified and researched many of the historical facts. Without her discipline, loyalty and hard work, this book would not have been produced.

The excellent copy-editing was the work of Ahmad Thomson.

The motif used throughout the book as a chapter opener is based on a Qur'anic verse from Sūrat al-Anbiyā and translates as 'We sent thee not, save as a mercy for all peoples'. It is reproduced by kind permission of the Iraqi Cultural Centre Gallery.

INTRODUCTION

Sufism and Islam cannot be separated, in the same way that higher consciousness or awakening cannot be separated from Islam. Islam is not an historical phenomenon that began 1,400 years ago. It is the timeless art of awakening by means of submission. Sufism is the heart of Islam. It is as ancient as the rise of human consciousness.

In this work, we attempt to present an overview of the meaning of Sufism. We describe its origins and practices, and the historical background out of which Sufism, as it is known today, arose in the East and then spread throughout the rest of the world. We also attempt to show that the Sufis are the upholders of the real message of Islam. Sufism only arises when abuse of Islam is rampant. Otherwise, Sufism and real Islam are one and the same.

The rise of Sufism began after the first century of Islam as a struggle against the increasing distortions and misrepresentations of its teachings, especially as perpetrated by the leadership of the day. Rulers or kings could often be seen to be using the name of Islam to justify their own ends, or to be discarding those aspects of its teachings which did not suit their purposes or extravagant lifestyle. It is from this time onwards that history records the growing revival, renewal and militancy among many groups of sincere Muslims throughout the expanding Muslim world who were eager to restore the pure and original message brought by the Prophet Muhammad.

This was a spontaneous awakening of individuals discovering the true prophetic way who were inspired by the inner light of awakening and fulfilment. Sufism spread across the land without its being a centrally organised movement. The Sufi brotherhood was a reality without much of an outer co-ordination or organisation. Its reality was the awakening of the original ascetic and joyful qualities within people's hearts and the acceptance of the outer prophetic law. Sufism bore similarities to ascetic mysticism, yet it also allowed for spiritual militancy in many instances. The brotherhood which was experienced by the Sufis was due mostly to their inner conditioning and state of their hearts, rather than to adherence to any particular theological doctrine or other ethnic or traditional bondages.

The Sufi movement in Islam echoed similar movements in other major religions, such as Cabbalism in Judaism, Gnosticism or Unitarianism in Christianity and, in a way, the advent of Buddhism where Hinduism is concerned. Also, as with other spiritual movements and revivals, we find instances of some Sufis taking things to extremes, and even distorting the multi-dimensions of Islam. Excess esotericism, or the rejection of the bounds of outer behaviour or the balanced prophetic way, are examples of this phenomenon, although they are the exception rather than the rule.

What is relevant to us today about Sufism is that it has maintained a clear thread and line of direct transmission of wisdom back to original Islam. The key to Sufism is that of inner awakening, freedom and joy through recognition of outer restriction by choice and discrimination. The numerous studies which are currently being published in an attempt to understand and predict the direction of the Islamic revival, such as the studies on the Sufis of Russia or on the Sufi brotherhoods in certain Middle Eastern countries, and so on, are all based on the fears of the various governments concerned of a revival which will place the leadership of the Muslims in the hands of those who are closest to emulating and living the way of life of the Prophet Muhammad. And this, of course, is a great threat to the existing authorities in most of the so-called Muslim countries today.

The reason that the majority of current studies on Sufism are of little use in a practical sense is because of the nature of inner awakening itself, which is the core of Sufism. Writing books about inner awakening is only really possible if one has experienced it, just as understanding such books is only really possible if one genuinely desires, or has already attained, such awakening. The Sufi is the locus of connecting the outer, physical reality with a timeless, spaceless dimension which is experienced within the self. The Sufi lives like the tip of the iceberg which is apparent in the seen world, while experiencing aspects of the hidden and veiled world which is the foundation of what is visible, and which forms the rest of its reality. He does his best to understand the causal, physical outer life while awakening to an immense inner Reality, which encompasses both the known and the unknown worlds, the unitive Reality of the seen and the unseen, of time and space and non-time-space.

It is for this reason that the inner life of the Sufi has no bounds, and yet he acknowledges and accepts the outer bounds with courtesy towards nature and the natural creation. The Sufi is totally content with the immeasurable bliss within. Yet he struggles outwardly towards a better quality of life on earth and does his best without being overly concerned about the ultimate results. Outer struggle and work are necessary companions to inner purification and contentment.

Genuine Sufis are essentially similar wherever they come from, in that they share an inner light and awakening, and an outer courtesy and service to humanity. Apparent differences between Sufis tend to relate to matters concerning spiritual practices or prescriptions for the purification of hearts. The sweet fruit of Sufism is the same. It is only the trees which may look different and which may flower in different seasons.

In this work, we have tried to show that those who claim that it is possible to have Sufism without Islam are only looking at one side of the story. Inner purity is generally attainable, but without its being contained outwardly, it will not result in any real flourishing of a spiritual culture or an enlightened environment. Inner light and joy may be sufficient for an individual living in a cave, but once we start interacting with others, we need to know where and what the bounds are for that social interaction to be able to take place, and this is where we find that the laws of Islam are necessary and inseparable from Sufism.

So the relevance of Sufism today is greater than it has been in any other age, for nowadays we can across cultural and political boundaries much more easily, because of ease of access through communications, travel and the closeness of the world. The message of Sufism is more urgent now, especially due to the fact that the world is increasingly becoming bound by materialism and consumerism. The awakening to the inner life of man is a necessary condition of his fulfilment as a human being. It comes as the pinnacle of his struggle with the elements and the fulfilment of his basic needs. Once our outer needs are met, then the inner must also be fulfilled. The two are so interlinked that those who are awakened to both the outer and inner realities see them as inseparable and continuous in the one creational, unific truth. The heart of such an awakened being reflects the entire universe, and such a being is described by the Sufi master, Ibn Arabi, in these words:

> My heart has become capable of every form:
> It is a pasture for gazelles,
> And a monastery for Christian monks,
> And a temple for idols,
> And the pilgrim's Ka'ba,
> And the tablets of the Torah,
> And the Book of the Qur'an.
> I follow the religion of Love:
> Whatever way Love's camel takes,
> That is my religion and my faith.

Shaykh Fadhlalla Haeri,
London, 1990

1 · DEFINITIONS OF SUFISM

The term Sufism, which has become over the ages very popularly used, and often with a wide range of meanings, originates from three Arabic letters *sa, wa* and *fa*. There have been many opinions on the reason for its origin from *sa wa fa*. According to some the word is derived from *safa* which means purity. According to another opinion it is derived from the Arabic verb *safwe* which means those who are selected. This meaning is quoted frequently in Sufi literature. Some think that the word is derived from the word *saf* which means line or row, implying those early Muslims who stood in the first row in prayer or supplication or holy war. Yet others believe that it is derived from *suffa* which was a low verandah made of clay and slightly elevated off the ground outside the Prophet Muhammad's mosque in Medina, where the poor and good-hearted people who followed him often sat. Some assume that the origin of the word Sufism is from *suf* which means wool, which implies that the people who were interested in inner knowledges cared less about their outer appearances and often took to wearing one simple garment all the year round which was made of wool.

Whatever its origin, the term Sufism has come to mean those who are interested in inner knowledge, those who are interested in finding a way or practice towards inner awakening and enlightenment.

It is important to note that this term was hardly ever used in the first two centuries of Islam. Many critics of the Sufis, or their enemies, remind us that this term was never heard of during the lifetime of the Prophet Muhammad, or of the people who came after him, or of the people who came after them.

However, during the second and third centuries following the advent of Islam in 622 some people began to call themselves Sufis, or to use other similar terms related to Sufism which meant that they were following the path of self-purification, the purification of the 'heart', and the improvement of the quality of their character and behaviour in order to reach the station of those who worship God as if they see Him, knowing that although they do not see Him, He sees them. This is what the term Sufism came to mean throughout the ages within the Islamic context.

I quote below a few great Sufi masters' definitions:

Imam Junayd of Baghdad (d. 910) defines Sufism as 'adopting every higher quality and leaving every low quality'. Shaykh Abu'l Hasan ash-Shadhili (d. 1258), the great North African spiritual master, defines Sufism as 'the practice and the training of the self through adoration and worship to return the self to the path of Lordship'. Shaykh Ahmad Zorruq (d. 1494) of Morocco defines Sufism as

> the science by means of which you can put right the 'heart' and make it exclusive to Allah, using your knowledge of the way of Islam, particularly jurisprudence and its related knowledges, to improve your actions and keep within the bounds of the Islamic Law in order for wisdom to become apparent.

He also adds: 'Its foundation is the knowledge of Unity, and you need thereafter the sweetness of trust and certainty, otherwise you will not be able to bring about the necessary healing of the "heart".' According to Shaykh Ibn Ajiba (d. 1809),

> *Sufism* is a science by means of which you learn how to behave in order to be in the presence of the ever-present Lord through

2

purifying your inner being and sweetening it with good actions. The path of *Sufism* begins as a science, its middle is actions and its end is divine gifts.

Shaykh as-Suyuti said, 'The Sufi is the one who persists in purity with Allah, and good character with creation.'

From many of the recorded sayings and writings on Sufism such as these, it can be concluded that the basis of Sufism is the purification of the 'heart' and safeguarding it from any affliction, and that its end product is the correct and harmonious relationship between man and his Creator. So the Sufi is the one whom God has enabled to purify his 'heart' and to establish his relationship with Him and His creation through treading upon the correct path, as best exemplified by the Prophet Muhammad.

Within its traditional Islamic context, Sufism is based on courtesy which ultimately leads to universal courtesy and awareness. Courtesy starts with the outer, and the true Sufi practises the outer cleansing and keeping within the bounds of what is permitted by God. It starts with following the Islamic Law, that is, by upholding the appropriate laws and requirements of Islam, which means the path of submission to God. So Sufism begins with acquiring the knowledge of the outer practices in order to develop, evolve and enliven the inner awakened state.

It is erroneous to imagine that a Sufi can end up with the fruits of Sufism, which are inner light, certainty and knowledge of Allah, without having maintained an outer protective shell which is based upon adherence to the requirements of the outer laws. This correct outer behaviour – physical behaviour – is based on making supplications and doing the prayers and all the other ritual acts of worship established by the Prophet Muhammad in order to achieve watchfulness of the 'heart', with its accompanying moods and states. Then one can progress on the purification ladder from one's base intentions towards higher aspirations, from the awareness of greed and pride towards humility and noble contentment. This inner work needs to be continued in a well-contained and maintained outer situation.

2 · THE EARLY DEVELOPMENT OF SUFISM

Al-Kindi (d. tenth century) refers to the appearance of a small community in Alexandria in Egypt in the ninth century which enjoined good and spoke out against evil. They were called Sufis. According to Muruj adh-Dhahab al-Mas'udi, Sufis first appeared during the time of the Abbasid caliph al-Ma'mun. According to Abu'l-Qasim Qushayri, the Sufis appeared in the ninth century, about two hundred years after the death of the Prophet Muhammad. The question arises, why did it apparently take so many years for people to take serious interest in the inner sciences? A brief retrospective glance at the early history of Islam may shed some light on this matter.

Let us transpose ourselves to Arabia at the beginning of the seventh century AD. What we find is a society of disunited Arab tribes who for centuries had been involved in an established tradition of warfare, idol-worship and other tribal values. Although the Arabs of that time engaged in commerce outside Arabia, they were little influenced by other cultures. The Byzantine Empire and the forays of Nebuchadnezzar into Arabia really had little impact upon them. So we find a people who had been carrying on their traditional nomadic way of life for centuries with little change. Suddenly an incredible 'Prophetic Light' manifests before them. This light begins to clearly identify and destroy the inhumanities and injustices in their society.

The incredible being who brought this new light of knowledge was the Prophet Muhammad. For twenty-three years Muhammad sang the eternal truth that man is born into this world in order to learn the ways of creation while journeying back to his source, the One Creator, for although man is free in his essence he is constrained and restricted by the outer laws that govern existence.

Muhammad spoke the same eternal truth which was spoken by thousands of divine messengers before him, and he spoke it in the contemporary language of his land, a language which was the highest cultural achievement of and a gift to those people. The Arabs had no other artistic heritage other than their language. The Prophet expounded the eternal truth to a people who had been immersed in the darkness of brutal ignorance for centuries. After years of effort, he had gathered a handful of supporters, most of whom had been persecuted and forced to flee to Ethiopia to seek protection under a benign Christian ruler called the Negus. Having withdrawn from Mecca to Medina in AD 622 – the point from which Muslim dating begins, and the event which is known as the Hijra – Muhammad established a new community of people from different parts of Arabia, but chiefly from Mecca and Medina. This community's outward orientation during worship of Allah was the Ka'aba, a cube-shaped building made of stone which was originally erected by the Prophet Abraham in Mecca, but its day-to-day orientation was the blessed Prophet himself. They followed this being, his teachings and his explanations of the Qur'anic injunctions which were revealed to him, inwardly orientated to their Creator. They worshipped Allah and followed the Prophet who lived by knowledge and love of Allah.

In the last ten years of the Prophet's life, and especially during the last three years, events began to move quickly. During this period, thousands of bedouins whose tendency was to go where power and victory prevailed, saw Islam dominating their land more and more, and accordingly they all embraced Islam in their thousands. When Muhammad died, the nascent Muslim community suffered a great shock which resulted in a hasty and tense election of Abu Bakr as the first leader of the community.

The Prophet Muhammad had indicated on numerous occasions to whom the Muslims should refer about matters concerning the way of Islam after his death, like a responsible doctor who, when about to go on leave or retire, tells his patients to whom they should refer in his absence. A doctor knows his patients' condition better than anyone else. It was quite natural for a spiritual master like Muhammad to point out who was best suited to run the affairs of the community after his death, in accordance with the divine laws which had been revealed to him. However, a disagreement arose as to whether the Prophet had specifically appointed Imam Ali as his successor, or whether he had simply mentioned him as the greatest among them in knowledge and virtue. The outcome was that before the Prophet was buried, the Arabs started lobbying for power. Those who were from Medina wanted to elect one from among themselves as their leader. At the last moment, two of the closest companions of the Prophet, Abu Bakr and Umar, managed to join the circle and, with the support of Umar, Abu Bakr was elected as leader of the community, being the respected elder and acknowledged sincere companion of the Prophet.

Abu Bakr's leadership lasted for two years, a period which was full of internal strife. The Arab psyche does not like to be subjugated in any way, for theirs is a free-spirited mentality. One common method of subjugation is the compulsory paying of tax money to another. The paying of the Islamic alms tax, which Abu Bakr enforced in the case of those who refused to pay it, was interpreted by some as being a form of subjugation to which they did not wish to submit. Thus most of the tribes who had recently joined the Islamic movement suddenly found that they had to pay up and actually give something away, rather than simply benefiting from the booty. This was a cause of dissension within the rapidly expanding Muslim community. Besides this, there were false claimants to prophethood and Abu Bakr's period of leadership was mostly spent in suppressing internal strife.

After the death of Abu Bakr in 634, Umar, who had already been appointed by Abu Bakr as his vice-regent, became the next leader of the Muslim community. During the ten years of his leadership there was a vast expansion of Islam. Egypt and the Persian and Byzantine Empires were conquered, including Jerusalem, the keys of which were given to Umar in person by the Christians. Umar was exemplary in his simplicity and lived most frugally. He was fatally stabbed by a Persian slave whilst praying in the mosque in 644.

The next leader, Uthman, was appointed by a group of people who had been selected by Umar to choose his successor. He came from the Ummayad clan, some of whose members had been arch-enemies of the Prophet. Many of the Ummayads had only embraced Islam after the conquest of Mecca by the Prophet and his followers, when they felt that there was no other option left for them. They accepted Islam reluctantly, and largely continued to live in the manner to which they had been accustomed in the past. Uthman himself did not care much for worldly matters, but allowed many members of his clan to live as they wished. He appointed many members of the Ummayad clan to key positions in the governance of the newly acquired Muslim territories, and accordingly there are those who have accused him of nepotism. In the first six years of his leadership there was continued territorial expansion by the Muslims, as well as consolidation of the lands which had already been conquered. In reality, however, it was the start of a reversal to rulership by men of greed rather than a continuation of Islamic governance by men of spiritual knowledge and piety.

During the rule of Uthman, which lasted for twelve years, many of the Muslims fell back considerably into the pre-Islamic way of ignorance, superstitions and tribalism. The booty from the Persian, Byzantine and Egyptian Empires poured into Mecca and Medina, resulting in an era of opulent decay and frivolity. Large houses and palaces began to be constructed during this period. One architect at this time was Abu Lu'lu, the Persian slave who had murdered Umar because Umar had imposed a substantial tax on him. In Umar's time, a house had usually consisted of a small square plot of land on which two or three rooms were built. On one side of these rooms was a courtyard, in the middle of which was a well, and in the corner a container for storing grain. It was all built on one level. However, during the time of Uthman, many palaces were built, and people began to vie with each other in constructing grander buildings.

After Uthman's murder in 656, which occurred while he was reciting the Qur'an, Imam Ali was popularly elected as the next leader of the Muslims. His rule lasted for nearly six years and was full of internal strife and warfare. By that time many people called themselves Muslims but did not totally know or imbibe the Muhammadan way of life. We find Muslims swearing by the Qur'an, but going against its real meaning. In the year 656 the first mass swearing to a lie took place. The Prophet had warned his wife, Ayesha, that one day she would find herself fighting on the wrong side, and would thereby commit the worst grievance, in a place called Hawab, and that the dogs of Hawab would bark at her. Many years later, while passing by this place on her way to the battle of Jamal to fight against Imam Ali, she heard the barking of dogs and remembered the prophetic warning. She asked what the place was called and was told that it was Hawab. However some of her companions brought forty so-called Muslims to swear falsely on the Qur'an that it was not Hawab. Again, during the battle of Siffin in 657, another incident of falsely swearing on the Qur'an took place.

After Imam Ali's martyrdom in 661, in which he was fatally stabbed while in prostration during the prayer, his son Imam Hasan was in a natural and deserved position to be the next leader of the Muslims. However Mu'awiya, the Ummayad governor of Syria who was trying to secure the position of ruler for himself and his clan, began to incite people against Imam Hasan. Imam Hasan had a large army at his disposal. He knew the weaknesses of his people and did not want dissension within his army. He also realised the cleverness and treachery of Mu'awiya. He did not wish to see the blood of Muslims futilely shed. So he accepted a truce offered by Mu'awiya whereby he gave up any claim to the leadership of the Muslims without relinquishing his exalted spiritual station. Just like Imam Ali, who had not simply sat aside when he was not elected as the first Muslim leader, but had done his best to put right what was going wrong during the years of his predecessors' rule, so Imam Hasan had no other option than to accept the fact that although he was the best of people at that time, yet he could not lead the Muslims. His acceptance of the truce was not a relinquishment of his true spiritual station, but rather an indication of it. Since it was not possible to translate his inner greatness into an outer statesmanship without having Muslim kill Muslim, the only alternative was to accept the conditions of the truce, which also stipulated that after him his brother Imam Husan would be the next leader of the Muslims. However Mu'awiya very cleverly reneged on all the terms of the truce after the murder of Imam Hasan in 661, and appointed his decadent son Yazid to be his successor. Accordingly Imam Husayn revolted against Mu'awiya and Yazid.

Imam Husayn was invited by the people of Kufa in Iraq to join them and was promised great support against Mu'awiya. The Kufans were a new community with fewer vested interests than the people of Mecca and Medina. By this time, Mecca had become an important centre for producing wine and music, and dancing girls were the order of the day. In pre-Islamic times, Arabs had honoured prostitutes who often sat on the same chair as an Arab ruler and gave him advice. This tradition had been revived in the time of Mu'awiya, and even though Kufa was a new city with a new Muslim community, some of its inhabitants had also reverted back to the old ways of the pre–Islamic period, although they did not have the traditions of the desert and the backwardness of the nomadic bedouins. Despite this situation, several thousand physically strong Kufans voiced their support for Imam Husayn and wanted him to lead them. Accordingly Imam Husayn marched towards Kufa to continue his secular and spiritual leadership.

When he was half way to Kufa, Imam Husayn received the news that his emissary had been killed by the soldiers of Yazid. He had no alternative but to continue his journey. Yazid's troops intercepted him and insisted that he acknowledge the leadership of Yazid, who was known to be a drunkard who openly flouted the laws of Islam. Imam Husayn had no option but to fight against such a betrayal and corruption of Islam. In the ensuing battle of Kerbala, about seventy-two members of his family were martyred, including babies and children who either died of thirst or from their enemies' arrows. In the end, Imam Husayn was martyred and beheaded. The surviving women and members of his family were dragged in chains and made to walk across the burning desert to Damascus, where they were brought to the court of Yazid.

The battle of Kerbala in 661 marked an important turning point in the history of Islam. It served as a pointed reminder to those Muslims who had abandoned the unitive path of Islam to return to it. The way of Islam was revived by the death of Imam Husayn since it reminded many people of the need to follow spiritual leadership, and not merely the worldly rule of greedy kings, and to honour the sovereignty of Allah on this earth by following in the footsteps of the Prophet Muhammad. It also reminded the people that whoever was chosen as a temporal ruler should also be the most qualified person spiritually: he should be the most evolved person in consciousness, pious, humble and accessible to people, in order to uplift them, and not a ruler over them who, while living in affluence and luxury, terrorised them.

It was during this time that many of the present-day Muslim customs and habits originated. Within seventy years of Muhammad's death, most of the basic Islamic tenets and teachings were being ignored by many so-called Muslims, although of course there were also those who embodied and understood this noble teaching. Thus many of the so-called cultural and ethnic habits that we see in Muslims today are not derived from the original teachings of Islam, but trace their origins back to that period of the corrupt Ummayad dynasty. Indeed dynastic rule itself was forbidden by Muhammad. The separation of men and women within the same house began in Damascus. There were men who wanted to have dancing girls in their palaces and so they created for the women of the household ladies' quarters in order to separate them from the men's quarters, which had not existed in houses before.

The mosque, which had been the centre of the community where the general public met, and which was the centre of economic, social and political exchange as well as a place of worship, ceased to be so. The mosque became a place of ritualistic worship and lost its pivotal position in the life of the community. The caliph grew fat, often drank and did not want to leave his palace. Accordingly the palace became the centre of power and government activities. In order not to have his debauchery openly exposed, the caliph separated the women and the children from himself, and thus the home was divided and fragmented.

During this period of corrupt Ummayad rule, more conquests were taking place and more and more people were embracing Islam. On the whole, however, the rulers were mostly oppressive and worldly, and although there were many sincere and wise Muslims who understood and embodied the teachings of Islam, they were prevented from actually governing their communities by those who were hungry for power and wealth. Occasionally, a decent ruler would emerge, such as an eighth-century ruler called Umar ibn Abd al-Aziz (d. 717) who ruled for only two years. During this period he revived the original teaching of the blessed Prophet and stopped people from cursing Imam Ali and the family of the Prophet from the pulpit in the mosques. However rulers such as he were the exception rather than the general rule.

Sincere and pious Muslims could not tolerate injustice and oppression indefinitely, and there emerged a movement led by Abu Muslim Khurasani committed to re-establishing justice and the true way of Islam. To begin with, it was a popular revolutionary movement against the Ummayads in favour of the Hashimites and the immediate family of the Prophet. However, when the cause was won, and the Ummayad dynasty was brought to an end in 749, the rulership of Muslim society was usurped by the Abbasids on the pretext of their being related to the family of Muhammad, although the connection was remote.

So by the year 750 another dynastic rulership had been established. In the years that followed, it was not unusual for a king to order some members of his family to be killed in order to end a power struggle or to remove any possible contender for his position. For example, Ma'mum killed his brother Amin, his rival to the Abbasid throne. Some women were engaged in trickery behind the scenes, and kings aspired to become emperors and live in luxury and opulence. This was the prevailing situation in Muslim society only two hundred years after the advent of Islam. There is no doubt that there also existed people of great wisdom and virtue and seekers after truth, as well as well-meaning scholars and men of knowledge and light, in the Muslim community, but on the other hand, we find tyrannical and decadent Abbasid kings who called themselves rulers and yet distorted the Muhammadan model. There were many attempts by Muslims to bring the unjust caliphate to an end, but most of these were unsuccessful. Zayd ibn Ali and many others revolted against their unjust rulers, but they were put to the sword.

It was these circumstances of blatant political and social contradictions that gave rise to the emergence of the Sufis, pious and thoughtful Muslims under the general umbrella of Islam, wanting to distinguish themselves from the ruling party and their worldly supporters. So we find the Sufi movement beginning as a natural consequence of Muslim society accepting and following corrupt dynastic rulership rather than following the King of kings, Allah the Almighty, through following his true representatives on this earth.

Muslims who were aware of the real prophetic teachings, but unable to change the existing situation, started devoting their life to prayers and the discipline of inner purification. Imam Ali Zayn al-Abidin, the son of Imam Husayn, is just one of many prominent examples. These Muslims could not turn their energy outwardly against the evil regimes, so they were compelled to turn it inwardly against the evil within the human self. These are the people who later came to be called the Sufis.

Another group who gathered round the spiritual leaders who were descended from the Prophet Muhammad, in order to receive the true teachings of Islam, also rejected the caliphs and kings who prolonged corrupt dynastic rule. They were called the Shi'a, which means the followers, the party, the group, or the partisans.

12

The title of Imam was not only used by both of these groups to denote a qualified and recognised spiritual leader, but also, in the Shi'a Islamic tradition, the term took on an added meaning, being used to designate twelve particular spiritual masters who are descended from the Prophet Muhammad. Each master, in his lifetime, confirmed the qualifications of and named his successor, the next Imam. In Sufi orders, a similar designation was accorded to the head of the order. The title of Shaykh, or spiritual master, could only be conferred by a recognised Shaykh upon another.

Whereas the Shi'as simply refused to follow the kingly caliphs and generally isolated themselves, the Sufis tolerated these rulers, saying that they could not deny their actual existence and therefore they had to abide by the laws of society and its ruler. However they sought inner enlightenment and adopted the Sufi path. From the Sufi point of view, it is said that if you cannot change the kings, then change yourself. If you cannot change the government, then change your lower self that is governing you individually from within.

What the first Sufis did can be done by anyone who is seeking the higher meaning in life. Hence it is superficial to say that Sufism came into existence two hundred years after the Prophet Muhammad's death, or that it originated from the poor and good-hearted simple people who were among the earliest followers of the Prophet. Both these views are true as well as false. Sufism is a movement that began to take form, identity and size when Islamic leadership or rulership deviated from the original teachings of Islam. It was at this stage that the Sufi circles began to grow. These circles became a sign of protection as well as a sign of identity which differentiated between a real Muslim (that is, a Sufi) and the one who deviated from the original Muhammadan code.

The Shi'as, as already noted earlier, did not accept the generally held opinion of most Muslims that, as regards a corrupt regime, to have a tyrant ruler is better than having anarchy. So whenever it was possible, the Shi'as tried to do away with unjust rulers and in turn they were often massacred. The Sufis, as we have already seen, addressed themselves to man's inner problems and, therefore, developed the science of the self. When Imam Junayd was asked, 'When did the name *Sufi* originate?' he said, 'Sufism was a reality without a name, but now in our time, it is a name without a reality.'

Throughout the history of Islamic civilisation, we occasionally find a Sufi master rising to denounce openly a regime which has deviated from the original Muhammadi path to an unacceptable degree. A true Sufi does not accept the esoteric path only, because he is a man of Unity. He does not separate the inner from the outer. He distinguishes between them and recognises where one stops and the other begins. He does not say that he is solely a person of the inner and become a recluse. The Sufi spiritual masters were not recluses. They had the vision of totality. From the Sufi point of view, if you start at one end you end up at the other end. If you start with outer purity, you end up at the other end by purifying your inner self. If you start by purifying your inner self, you end up being concerned with the outer and with society.

If you want to know why a tree is so big and robust and can withstand the onslaught of hurricanes, you have to dig deep in order to discover the depth of its roots. One reflects the other and traces the story of the other. If you want to have a strong outer situation, then you need a strong inner situation. For example, a galleon or sailing ship carrying a full cargo will only cross the tumultuous seas if it has a strong mast and a very large sail. In the same way, the Sufis were saying, the more involved a person is in a worldly situation, the more concerned and involved he ought to be in a spiritual situation. Then there is a balance. You cannot have the one without the other. This is the meaning behind the observation that he who is seeking the world is in reality seeking a spiritual one, but he is unaware of it. The greedy person is in need of security. However the ultimate real security is inner contentment and certainty. If he seeks it outwardly, it is because the outer quest is easier. It is gross and physical and therefore more tangible and workable. The inner is more subtle and difficult to work. He who is arrogant outwardly is actually insecure inwardly, which is why he puts on a show of arrogance. He who is inwardly insecure protects himself by outwardly elevating himself.

14

These are the laws of the self which were discussed, taught and practised in the Sufi circles. This does not mean that they were not known before this time and that they emerged only two hundred years after the Prophet's lifetime. These types of knowledge were known both before and during the time of Muhammad and practised without being formalised or labelled. It is like someone cooking a meal and eating it without having any name for the dish or a recipe book. So Sufism existed at the time of the Prophet without that label actually being given to it. That is the meaning of Imam Junayd's saying, 'Sufism was a reality without a name.' It was not an objective science to be studied by orientalists and analysed and disseminated by linguists. There is a big difference between merely collecting recipes and actually cooking and eating. Nowadays there are hardly any real cooks anywhere, but there are many people who collect and exchange recipes, such as 'There was an emergence of Sufism in the ninth century', which does not mean anything if one contemplates deeply. Statements that Sufism emerged two centuries after Muhammad's lifetime are superficial unless one considers the backdrop of the political history of Islam. For a reflective mind, it becomes quite clear that the emergence of Sufism out into the open was a reaction to the oppressive and unjust external situation caused by the ruling party which had deviated from the original Islamic way.

To highlight our previous comments, we see that within fifty years after Muhammad's death, not only do we have a reversal of the Muslim situation back to racism, feudalism and a class system of the haves and have-nots, together with the earlier pre-Islamic Arab family and tribal social structures, but also we see that the situation was now worse than in pre-Islamic times because of the confidence which the new religion had given the Arabs. Now that these people were the rulers, they used the frontal protection of the name of Islam to hide behind and justify their actions.

Within a hundred years of Muhammad's death, even more changes had taken place within the new Islamic society. Religious teaching in the mosques began to take on a conventional form. In the time of the Prophet, the mosque was simple in its architecture. There were no minarets. The idea of the minaret was introduced at a later stage, since this was a good way of transmitting the sound of the call to prayer over a long distance. Gradually, the mosque grew more sophisticated in design. Alongside these developments, the teaching of the religion of Islam began to take place in an increasingly formalised way. People began teaching the Qur'an and the recorded actions and sayings of the Prophet and jurisprudence in a more formal, standardised manner. The emergence of the Sufis after the death of Muhammad was not to bring any new teaching, but simply to keep the spirit and original form of Islam, its full meaning and inner transmission, alive, rather than solely adhering to the formal aspects of the state religion which by then had begun to take shape. At the time of Muhammad's death, there were people who knew and understood the Qur'an and the recorded actions and sayings of the Prophet, and who were applying them in their lives. The sciences of religion which appeared later, such as theology and Qur'anic exegesis, hardly existed in these early days. Alongside the emergence of these theological sciences, the search for inner revival also began to take place. Previously they were not separate, and the real Muslims lived more simply and spontaneously.

Within a few hundred years of Muhammad's death, the political power of the Muslims started waning. Muslim Spain, which had been conquered in 756, was at this time beset with strife, largely because it too had settled for dynastic rule. There were power struggles and turmoil in Cordoba, rulers of small kingdoms throughout Andalusia were fighting against each other and Muslims were shedding the blood of Muslims. In the East, there was Abbasid decadence and internal division. The Fatimids, who were the rulers of Egypt, had also become politically weak. Most of the scholars of Sufism regard the pinnacle of the Sufi movement as having occurred around the tenth century. Mansur al-Hallaj, who was martyred in 923, is often referred to in this context.

It was during this period of social, political, spiritual and moral decadence and decline that the Sufi movement grew in strength to revive the true way of Islam, as has already been discussed earlier. In this sense, I regard the Sufi movement as a parallel to the prophethood of Jesus, whose message was not to destroy the Law of Moses, but to revive the spirit of the Law in order to rebalance it. As a result, we do not find Jesus changing the already existing Mosaic Law, but confirming it, while showing its true application and meaning. It was a later convert, Paul, and others, who brought about what is called Christianity. In the same way, it was during this period, in which many of the Muslims had lost sight of the true application and meaning of Islam, that major Sufi writings on spiritual and moral disciplines appeared in order to guide the people who desired balance, purity, self-knowledge and inner illumination.

One of the earliest documents on Sufism is that of Abdar-Rahman as-Sulami who was born in 938 in Nishapur, in present-day Iran. Nishapur at that time was a great centre of learning. As-Sulami, in accordance with the tradition of his day, memorised the Qur'an by heart, learned Arabic grammar and studied the recorded actions and sayings of the Prophet and the other theological sciences. Like any other person whose soul is not sufficiently nourished by conventional religious teaching, and who has the capability and means to nourish it further, he began to travel extensively, especially between Balkh and Bukhara. Those areas were at that time very much alive with spiritual teachers and awakened souls. As-Sulami travelled westwards and spent a considerable length of time in Baghdad, Cairo and Mecca. He collected the wisdom of as many Sufi saints as possible and compiled it in his work *Tabaqat as-Sufiyya*. This is the earliest collection of biographies of Sufis. It contains the biographies of more than a hundred Sufis whom he encountered during his travels. Many of the written works of the Sufi masters which he mentions in his book are no longer traceable. Accordingly this document of as-Sulami is an important historical account of what was happening in the Sufi world up to his day. In it, one finds out the situation regarding the search for truth and the revival of the inner meaning of the way of Islam, and the continuation of the transformative element of this way of life, during the ninth and tenth centuries.

As well as as-Sulami's work, there are other major works on Sufism, such as *Qut al-Qulub* by Abu Talib al-Makki (d. 996), *Risalah al-Qushayriyya* by Abu'l-Qasim al-Qushayri (d. 1072), *Ihya Ulum ad-Din* by Imam Abu Hamid al-Ghazzali (d. 1111), and the treatises of Abd al-Qadir al-Gilani (d. 1166), to name but a few. These works later became the basis of Sufi studies and the further development of the science of Sufism. In all these major Sufi works, there is a balanced teaching of both the outer code of conduct, or Islamic Law, and the inner reality of existence. These works, especially the *Ihya Ulum ad-Din*, were considered to be basic Sufi reference works for a long period of time, for they were the result of the transformative experience of those men and were used by them and their successors as a foundation course for teaching the science of Sufism. These men aimed at bringing about an awakening of human consciousness that resonated with or was close to the inward state of the Prophet Muhammad. The aim and the ultimate goal of Sufism in its formative as well as in its later years was none other than to strive to resonate with, or become like a tuning fork vibrating with, the same frequency as Muhammad.

The science of Sufism has always been directed towards emulating and embodying the Prophetic model, so as to be illuminated and transformed by its light, in a form which is clearly understandable experientially in a programmable way by a sincere follower. This may be achieved, for example, by starting with certainty through knowledge, which is obtaining information about the purpose of man's life on this earth and his ultimate destiny through theoretical knowledge, then progressing to certainty through vision, which is when knowledge begins to grow within oneself through one's personal experience, and then finally arriving at certainty through experiencing reality, which is knowledge through your own being, through your primal being, which is now activated.

3 · SUFI ORDERS

In the early centuries of Islam, the Sufis were not organised into particular circles or orders. However, as time went by, the teaching and personal example of Sufis living the spiritually decreed code of life began to attract many groups of people. Between the ninth and eleventh centuries, we find that various Sufi Orders, which included adepts from all strata of society, began to emerge. As these Sufi Orders, or brotherhoods, came into existence, the centre of Sufi activity was no longer the private house, school or work place of the spiritual master. A more institutional structure was given to their gatherings, and the Sufi Orders began to use centres which existed specifically for these gatherings. A Sufi centre was usually called a *khaneqah* or *zawiyya*. The Turks called their Sufi sanctuary a *tekke*. In North Africa such a centre was called a *ribat*, the name which was also used to describe the frontier fortresses of the Sufi soldiers who defended the way of Islam and fought against those who tried to destroy it. In the Indian sub-Continent a Sufi centre was called a *jama'at khana* or *khanegah*.

In the same way that the various schools of Islamic Law which emerged in the early centuries after the Prophet Muhammad's death were meant to define a clear path for the application of that law, so the Sufi Orders which emerged during the same period also intended to define a simple path for the practice of inner purification. In the same way that many great schools of Islamic Law ceased to be propagated and accordingly ended, likewise many great Sufi Orders faced a similar situation. During the ninth century, more than thirty schools of Islamic Law existed, but later on this number was reduced to five or six. During the twelfth century, you could not count the number of Sufi Orders, partly because there were so many, and partly because they were not yet defined as such. Most of the great spiritual masters and teachers of the Sufi Orders and schools of law did not expect that their teachings would be given a defined and often a rigid interpretation at a later stage after their deaths, or that the Sufi Orders and schools of law would be named after them. However, the preservation of the Sufi Orders was often partly a result of their physical isolation as well as the direction that mainstream Islam took.

A noticeable trend within these Sufi Orders is that many of them intermingled, often strengthening each other and at times weakening each other. Most of the Sufi Orders kept a record of their lineage, that is their chain of transmission of knowledge from master to master, which was often traced back to one of the Shi'ite spiritual leaders and accordingly back through Imam Ali to the Prophet Muhammad, as a proof of their authenticity and authority. The only exception to this is the Naqshbandi Sufi Order whose lineage of transmission of knowledge traces back through Abu Bakr, the first leader of the Muslim community in Medina, to Muhammad.

The following are a few of the Sufi Orders which are still established today, each with its own predominating characteristics. Seekers of knowledge can be members of one or more of the Sufi Orders, as indeed they often follow more than one spiritual master. The following are only a sample of those Sufi Orders with which the author has personal familiarity.

THE QADIRI ORDER

The Qadiri Order was founded by Shaykh Abd al-Qadir al-Gilani (d. 1166) from Gilan in Persia, who eventually settled in Baghdad in Iraq. After his death, his Sufi Order was propagated by his sons. The Qadiri Order has spread to many places, including Syria, Turkey, some parts of Africa such as Cameroun, the Congo, Mauritania and Tanzania, and in the Caucasus, Chechen and Ferghana in the Soviet Union, as well as elsewhere.

THE RIFA'I ORDER

Founded by Shaykh Ahmad ar-Rifa'i (d. 1182) in Basra, the Rifa'i Order has spread to Egypt, Syria, Anatolia in Turkey, Eastern Europe and the Caucasus, and more recently to North America.

THE SHADHILI ORDER

The Shadhili Order crystallised around Shaykh Abu'l-Hasan ash-Shadhili of Morocco (d. 1258) and eventually became one of the greatest Sufi Orders, having an extraordinarily large following. Today it is found in North Africa, Egypt, Kenya and Tanzania, the Middle East, Sri Lanka and elsewhere, including the West and North America.

THE MEVLAVI ORDER

The Mevlavi or Mawlawi Order centres around Mawlana Jalal ud-Din Rumi of Qonya in Turkey (d. 1273). Today it is mostly found in Anatolia in Turkey and more recently in North America. The followers of this order are also known as whirling dervishes.

THE NAQSHBANDI ORDER

The Naqshbandi Order takes its name from Shaykh Baha ud-Din Naqshband of Bukhara (d. 1390). It is widely spread in central Asia, the Volga, the Caucasus, the north-west and south-west of China, Indonesia, the Indian sub-Continent, Turkey, Europe and North America. This is the only known Sufi Order which traces the genealogy of its lineage of transmission of knowledge back through the first Muslim ruler, Abu Bakr, unlike the rest of the known Sufi Order which trace their origins back to one of the Shi'ite spiritual leaders, and therefore through Imam Ali, and so to the Prophet Muhammad.

THE BEKTASHI ORDER

The Bektashi Order was founded by Hajji Bektash of Khurasan (d. 1338). Shi'ite ideas strongly permeate this Sufi Order. It is limited to Anatolia in Turkey and was most powerful up until the early twentieth century. The order is regarded as a follower of Shi'a Islamic Law.

THE NI'AMATULLAH ORDER

The Ni'amatullah Order was founded by Shaykh Nur ud-Din Muhammad Ni'amatullah (d. 1431) in Mahan near Kirman in South-west Iran. Its followers are found mostly in Iran and India.

THE TIJANI ORDER

The Tijani Order was founded by Shaykh Abbas Ahmad ibn at-Tijani, an Algerian Berber (d. 1815). It has spread from Algeria to the south of the Sahara and into western and central Sudan, Egypt, Senegal, West Africa and northern Nigeria, as well as being represented in the West and in North America.

THE JARRAHI ORDER

The Jarrahi Order was founded by Shaykh Nur ud-Din Muham-mad al-Jarrah of Istanbul (d. 1720). It is limited mostly to Turkey, with some representation in the West and in North America.

THE CHISTI ORDER

The most influential Sufi Order in the sub-Continent of India and Pakistan has been the Chisti Order, which takes its name from Khwaja Abu Ishaq Shami Chisti (d. 966). Its spread has been primarily within south-east Asia.

Sufi Orders, like other movements, have tended to be cyclical in nature. A Sufi Order has generally had a cycle of two to three hundred years before weakening and decaying. Whenever there has been a need for it, a Sufi Order begins to rise, then reaches its climax, and then gradually declines and disintegrates.

One observable trend in the history of Sufism has been that whenever there has been a lack of Islamic source material, such as the Qur'an or the original way of Muhammad, within a Sufi Order, then it has tended to be dominated by the stronger and older culture of its environment. This adulteration is noticeable in the Chisti Order of south-east Asia and in the Sufi Orders of Indonesia which have integrated many elements of Hindu and Buddhist customs into their practices. Similarly the Sufi Orders of Africa below the region of Sudan have integrated some of the African tribal religious customs into their practices. All these Sufi Orders seem to have taken on some of the colour of cultishness in these remote regions.

4 · BASIC SUFI CONCEPTS

Like most aspects of the religion of Islam which became recorded and took on a formal aspect after the deaths of the Prophet Muhammad and the first four Muslim rulers, the different sciences related to the way of Islam also began to develop and grow in sophistication, such as the science of the Qur'an, the science of the recorded actions and sayings of Muhammad, the science of Islamic jurisprudence and all the other sciences concerned with theological studies. None of these sciences existed in any formal or structured manner in the early years of Islam, although the knowledge and wisdom on which they were based did exist.

The same trend of growth and complexification seems to have been repeated in the science of Sufism. From about a hundred years after Muhammad's death onwards, when people began to discriminate more and more between original Islam and pseudo-Islam, between spiritual Muslims and Muslims who supported dynastic monarchy, the various concepts of Sufism dealing with the purification of the self and the 'heart' began to manifest more prominently. This does not mean that these concepts and the practices which accompanied them did not exist in the first century of Islam. They were there, but they were far less structured, formulated or discussed. The early Muslims knew the meaning and reality of inner purity, reliance upon God, yearning and the actions based on that reliance and yearning which resulted in that purity, as well as the other basic Sufi concepts, but it was only later on that these concepts were discussed and recorded in a more structured way, in order to help the seeker on the path of knowledge, until he reached the point where he experienced subjectively what he had at first only learned about and accepted intellectually.

Belief generally begins with a possibility or a hypothesis. It can also be simply blind faith. Then comes the stage of experimentation. For example, in believing that death is not the end of life, one needs to assume that the story of life cannot be entirely physical. So an aspect of belief is that there is something else behind our physical existence. This very simple and ordinary starting point can become subjectively confirmed when it is personally experienced that the origin and source of life is beyond time and space, and that the body is a vehicle to reach higher consciousness. Belief is a force which drives one to progress along the spiritual path. In reality everyone is a believer, even if he calls himself a non-believer, because non-believing is in itself a state of belief. A person may believe that there is no other world, or experience after death. Such a belief too is a point from which a person is driven to derive maximum pleasure or happiness out of this life. In other words, everybody is a believer in something, and it is this belief which is a driving force along a path to fulfilment.

It is said in a tradition, 'The awakened one is a reflector of he who is on the path of awakening.' The basic concept which underlies the Sufi movement is the intention to bring about the development of the whole person, and not a fragment of a person, through correct belief, which some people have realised through enlightenment, based on practice and discipline. Thus the allegation that the Sufis are esotericists is incorrect. If some Sufis have emphasised esoteric teachings, it is because they judged that the priority need at the time was the science of understanding the self and inward purification. The real Sufi is not ignorant about the other dimensions of man, such as his role in society and in politics and in all matters pertaining to life in general. For man, according to the teachings of Sufism, is a microcosm of the totality of existence.

Sufism is none other than reliving the Muhammadan way of life. The early Shi'as had an advantage in having for 250 years qualified and recognised spiritual leaders from among the descendants of the Prophet to guide them in the Muhammadan way of life, in spite of their being persecuted by the Ummayad and Abbasid caliphs. However, most Shi'as concentrated more on learning the formal and ritualistic aspects of this lifestyle from these spiritual leaders, rather than its higher spiritual elements. Accordingly emphasis was placed on jurisprudence, and a relative neglect of philosophy and the science of the self is evident in any study of Muslim social history. However the way in which these spiritual leaders lived and the flexibility that they had as awakened Muslims are enough for us to see how real spiritual masters live. One such spiritual leader was brought near to the ruling caliph of the day. He was Imam Musa Rida. Another, who was imprisoned by the caliph, was Imam Musa ibn Ja'far. Another spiritual leader Imam Zayn al-Abidin, was given the opportunity to invite people to the way of Islam by means of his prayers and supplications. Yet another, Imam Ja'far as-Sadiq was surrounded by people who wanted to learn from him, and so he began to give structure to the sciences of jurisprudence and theology. These spiritual leaders were like different lamps giving off the same light, different representatives of the One God.

The Sufi is an enlightened being following the outer Islamic Law while his heart is encompassed by the inner Reality. However one cannot say much about Allah's ways for they are so numerous and some of them are strange. We find that some Sufis lean towards being recluses. Now Allah says through the Prophet Muhammad that those who are loved most by Allah are those who serve the creatures of Allah. We also observe that not every person who is enlightened can teach, just as not every person who is a scholar can be a great orator. Sometimes we find the reverse of the situation to be true in that a great religious orator has little real knowledge. Such people make a far greater impact on society than great scholars who do not have the gift of eloquence or the charisma. So a lack of communication from a quiet dervish or a Sufi does not reflect the extent of his knowledge or his true station.

We often find that spiritually oriented people need periods of meditation, prayer and seclusion. No prophet has ever attained prophethood without months or years of seclusion, often in caves. In the same way, the Sufis have followed in the footsteps of the prophets. They need periods of seclusion, periods of reducing the impact of the outer world on them in order to develop the inner. For example, one great spiritual master, called Shaykh Abu Madyan al-Maghribi (d. 1199), who eventually taught thousands of people, did not do so until he had spent some time in seclusion. It is said that he remained in his room for a year and did not go out except for the Friday prayer. People gathered at the door of his house and asked him to speak to them. When they pressed him, he went out. He saw some sparrows on a lotus tree. When the birds saw him they fled, and so he said. 'Had I been fit to speak to you, the birds would not have fled from me.' Then he returned and sat in his room for another year. The people came to him again. He went out and the birds did not flee from him, so he spoke to them and began to teach. If a person is spiritually evolved and is of an appropriate age with appropriate health and in an appropriate environment, then his wholeness is reflected wherever he is. He begins to teach as he lives his life fully, inwardly and outwardly, in a balanced way.

Sufism is primarily concerned with the 'heart' that reflects the truth which exists within it, beyond time and in time. The Sufi is the whole human being. He recognises that his reality is beyond time and space, and yet he understands that he himself is caught in his body in order to experience the duality of time and space in this world. The Sufi is the one who realises the courtesy due to the prison of his body which has been given to him on loan for a few years. He is aware of the fact that he is returning to the abode of infinite bliss from which he originally emerged. Sufism is an art of beingness through the attainment of divine knowledge. It is not an intellectual exercise for scholarly investigations and postgraduate studies.

As far as original Sufi works are concerned, they were not written in order to establish yet another school of Islamic law, like the Maliki, the Shafi'i and the Jafari schools of Islamic law for example, but they were written in order to help those who were already following the Sufi path. Studying the map and staying put is not the same as making the journey and using the map as you go along. The Sufi writings are helpful to the practitioners of the Sufi path, but the written word is a secondary experience compared to the direct benefits and transmission of knowledge which occur when the seeker keeps the actual company of a spiritual master. Writing is only useful as an aid, a memoir or a reminder for the practitioner. When such writings are discovered and taken and studied out of context, then confusion arises.

Let us consider, for example, the debate concerning the Unity of Being. Intellectuals question whether or not this concept is acceptable within the teachings of Islam and ask questions such as, 'What did Ibn Arabi mean by this term?' and 'Do other Sufis agree with him or not?' Such questions and the arguments which ensue are pitfalls and hindrances along the path of the true seeker, as well as being confusing for the general collective understanding of the spiritual process. I feel that there is no point in imitating and regurgitating the concepts or the statements that have come from other Sufi masters unless, that is, they are taken in their entire context and as an aid to the transmission of knowledge and wisdom. If Ibn Arabi has been of benefit to me in showing me the light that dazzled him, and obliterated his ego, and cleared away his doubts about Reality which had appeared to be clothed in duality, then I should be able to express such ideas in the language of my own time, because I am the product of a time which is different to that of Ibn Arabi. The blind utilisation of specific terminologies which were originally coined as part of a total ecosystem of Ibn Arabi or of other Sufis can only be done by those who have not attained their spiritual state or station, in which they simply described what they saw. Such people regurgitate what has already been digested by others. Even Imam Malik, founder of the Maliki school of Islamic Law, was faced with such a situation during his own lifetime, when many people were memorising and transmitting his book called *Al-Muwatta*. He emphasised that the work, which had taken fifty years to refine and complete, should not be passed on in a static fashion to semi-intelligent students in a hurry.

Ibn Arabi's unfoldment, for example, could serve our own unfoldment, as long as we are on the path of unfoldment. Each one of us has a unique set of fingerprints although all fingers perform the same functions. Taking certain Sufi terminology out of a special ecosystem is like stealing someone else's set of fingerprints. Besides which, those who are only engaged in discussing Sufism are not the same as those who are actually following the path of self-knowledge. Those who analyse and write about Sufism are not equal to those who are burning and yearning to receive divine nourishment. Generally speaking, most of the works written on Sufism by non-Sufis are hardly usable by practising seekers. There is a vast difference between these works and the work written by the Sufi masters themselves. A real Sufi can recognise the former work and knows that such work has come from the hand that does not produce nourishment.

Ibn Arabi says in his treatise on *The Limitlessness of the Reality* that 'No two things can happen twice in creation. If exactly the same pattern were to happen twice, then that would imply that Allah is limited.' Also, purely as a matter of commonsense and personal observation, we notice that there is no exact repetition in creation. Even if nothing else appears to have changed, the time has changed. If something happens which is very similar to what happened two hundred years ago, it still cannot be exactly the same happening. Although the issue or the setting may be the same, the weather, the environment and the people are not the same. Never is any instant, or any blink of an eye, like the one before it. It is all fresh, each moment. So by simply regurgitating what a particular Sufi has said or done in the past, one will not produce the same effect or result. However, one Sufi 'composer' may tune in to the music of another Sufi 'composer', for both have been able to produce their own music.

29

There are people who spend years trying to discover the structure and the system of the Sufi path of Mawlana Jalal' ud-Din Rumi, or of Imam Ali, by analysing their writings or recorded actions and sayings, without ever actually taking one step along that path. However for a real Sufi what matters is to be able to gain access to the actual state and station of the spiritual master. Some read about another's experience, and others have that experience.

As Imam Ja'far as-Sadiq has said, 'Do not expect your children to do what you did, because they belong to a different age.' One of the meanings of this is that although the meaning remains the same, the form, the system, the language and the behaviour will differ. Every Sufi is different to any other Sufi, and yet he is not different. He is different in his being in a different state or station or in a different culture to the others. He is not different in that, like the others, he is seeking the truth and is striving towards total awareness of Reality. So it is not Islamic philosophy or Sufi philosophy as such that is important for him, but what is pragmatic and practically usable. He longs to know the Absolute and he yearns for eternal love. He wants to know the unchanging state within himself by not being distracted or obsessed by the constantly changing situation outside. To be in such a station he needs a helping hand, a physician of the soul. The greatest physician for him is the blessed Prophet Muhammad. By having the Prophet as a model in his awareness, he then tries to find a living person who embodies the prophetic wisdom, both outwardly and inwardly, and who has more experience than himself of the Sufi path, to guide him. Sufi philosophical treatises are useful in discussions and debates, but in themselves they do not lead a person far along the divine path. Such a person needs a qualified guide.

5 · THE WAY OF THE SUFI

According to the way of the Sufis, a person who has attained the state of outer and inner awareness, and who has managed to reach a point of balance and centrality, is in a position to assist others and to reflect to them their own state of progress. Accordingly we find that throughout the ages the Sufis have kept close together. Spiritual masters accompany their close followers during all the stages of progress.

We need to distinguish between the two terms: *state* and *station*. It is the difference between how it is and where it's at. State means something which one can feel or taste. One can sometimes feel an inner state of incredible generosity or great upliftment. However this state may not be lasting. What is really desired by the seeker is to attain a station which cannot occur unless it is properly founded and secure. A station is not temporary and can always be relied upon and recalled. Most of the wayfarers on the path to Allah will taste different states to varying degrees of lasting without any permanence in them, which is unsatisfactory and insufficient. It is for this reason that a guiding hand is needed to ensure that a seeker becomes established in a desirable station. So the companionship and relating to people who are on the path is an essential factor in a seeker's progress. Another important reason for having the right companionship is that we are always a product of the last moment, and since this moment is born from the previous moment and that from the one before it, and so on, there is continuity. A person on his own cannot realise how much he has deviated from the path of self-knowledge or self-realisation. Thus a seeker needs a companion to reflect to him, like a mirror, his state and station.

Just as in the case of the physical or natural sciences where one would obviously tend to follow someone who has greater experience and qualifications in these sciences, so the same principle applies to the sciences of the self. On the physical level, we are constantly striving towards harmony and right action, and we follow those who have expertise in this field. In the same way, for inner harmony, the best qualified person is a real Sufi spiritual master. However, there is a difference between the outer and the inner sciences. In the outer sciences, the blemishes and imperfections are easily detectable. This is not the case with the inner sciences where, for example, a person can put a grin on his face whereas in reality he is very displeased within. Knowledge of the inner sciences requires a subtler specialisation. What is needed is a medicine for the 'heart', which is not easy to obtain or administer whereas physical healing is prescriptive, descriptive, analytical and logical, and therefore is easier to achieve.

Now to the question of whether it is best to follow only one spiritual master or many. Among the greatest men whom I have read about and met have been some who have followed many spiritual masters. Yet in reality the true follower of the path of enlightenment sees one spiritual master. The spiritual masters may differ in their exterior form and nature, but their inner reality is one and the same. One spiritual master may be very old and very quiet. Another may be young and dynamic. One may have taken on a politically active role, while another may not have done so. One may be economically productive and working on a farm. Another may be a scholar. One may be very sociable, while another may shun society and be more of a recluse, and so on. Their outer appearances and tendencies, like fingerprints, vary from one person to another, but a sincere seeker is not concerned with the outer. A seeker who has kept within the limits decreed by the outer laws is concerned most with inner development. The inner reality is to do with essence and source. When it comes to the source, there is oneness. When one moves further away from the source of light, one discriminates and sees different shadows and different colours and profiles. The closer one comes to the source of light, the less one sees the differences, until one is blinded and taken in and engulfed by the light itself. In other words, if a person has taken on a real spiritual master truly then he has in reality taken on all of the spiritual masters. It is a fallacy to think that one can discard one spiritual master and go to another, unless the first is not accomplished or is an imposter.

As the seeker evolves and moves forward, he can see himself being watched by his spiritual master and by those spiritual masters whom he meets through the courtesy of his own spiritual master. The intelligent seeker will always live and behave as though all of the spiritual masters whom he has met are watching over him, are actually with him and are his guides, warners and friends.

A major question that arises is how does a seeker find a real spiritual master? Or how can he be sure of the spiritual master's quality? The followers of the esoteric and inner traditions believe that Allah's mercy permeates and encompasses every situation and everything. The right teacher turns up at the right time if a person has sincerity and the right courtesy. The correct courtesy is patience and recognition of the need. And it is by divine mercy that the right answer comes at the right time for the seeker.

A true spiritual teacher must have the proper basic qualities, just as a physician is supposed to have fulfilled primary basic requirements before he can practise medicine. To begin with, a spiritual guide, that is a Sufi master, must be knowledgeable about all the outer aspects of the original way of Islam and its way of life. He must be fully conversant with the knowledge and practice of the way of Islam. He should apply what is in the Qur'an and the prophetic way of life to himself. If he has not practised the outer laws, how can he have practised the inner aspects of this way of life, let alone recommend others to practise them? So the true spiritual master must himself live the outer and inner codes of Islam fully.

Another condition of a spiritual master being a true teacher is that he must have achieved real enlightenment by arriving at complete knowledge of the self. The spiritual master must know the extraordinary vast horizon of the self. Whoever knows his self, truly he knows his Lord.

A true spiritual master must also have been given the express permission to start out and guide others on the path of self-knowledge, by another enlightened and experienced teacher who himself had been given permission to teach, and so on, back to the Prophet Muhammad. For there are people who keep within the outer limits of the Islamic Law, others who have achieved self-knowledge, and still others who have attained gnosis as well as the knowledge of the self, and yet they are unable to guide others. Just as it is not enough for a physician to have only studied and passed examinations, and observed and assisted other physicians in their work, before he himself can begin to practise medicine in his own right. He must also be given the permission or licence to practise medicine by a qualified physician who is satisfied with his ability to do so.

Another prerequisite is that there should be a seeker to receive knowledge from the spiritual master, just as there has to be a patient before a physician can practise his medicine. Finally, just as it is of no use for a physician to attend to a sick person if he is unable or unwilling to accept the remedy for his illness, so there is no need of a spiritual master if the seeker is not keen to follow him.

Now we come to the relationship between the seeker and the teacher. The extent to which a sick person benefits from the physician depends upon the extent of his trust in the prescribed medication and his diligence in following the prescription. The same principle, only magnified, applies to the science of self-knowledge and Sufism. Ultimately it is fineness and subtlety of understanding between the spiritual master and the close follower that matters. The extent of their real connection dictates the speed at which the seeker takes in and absorbs the colour and meaning of the spiritual master. The teacher is like a tuning fork, and if the close follower allows himself totally to vibrate in resonance with him, that is to follow his teacher completely, then he will soon sing the same song as his spiritual master. This does not happen immediately. It can develop and evolve by questioning, testing and adjusting, until the seeker trusts the teacher completely. A time comes when total commitment has to be made. The seeker will enter into a contract which is called initiation.

The ceremony of initiation has become quite a significant event in many Sufi Orders. Many pseudo-sufis have also adopted it and have further embellished it and ascribed mystical value to it. One example of this is the secret practices of the Freemasons. In this group, when a member reaches a certain level within the 'order', he is buried alive for a while in a coffin, symbolically implying the personal experience of death while still being in this life. After a while he is released from the coffin and 'brought back' to this existence. The Prophet Muhammad said, 'Die before you die,' meaning practise detachment and freedom before the final event of leaving your body happens.

The foundation of initiation is a bond or contract that draws the teacher and the taught together. It is an unwritten contract and therefore takes the form of an oath of allegiance. The seeker agrees to obey the teacher, and the teacher agrees to look after the close follower's progress and to guide him.

The reverse of initiation, which is casting out, also occurs sometimes when the teacher and the pupil reach a point whereby the bond between the two becomes invalid and the relationship is dead. At times the seeker renounces the teacher and highlights all that appears to be objectionable in the teacher. The anger of the seeker causes him to see all the negative aspects of the relationship and the apparently, to him, needless sacrifices he has made. As far as the real teacher is concerned, the seeker who leaves in anger is another victim of the lower self in man.

The degree of sophistication and the complexities of the rules of initiation seem to depend much upon the disposition of the spiritual master himself, and on his environment. Some spiritual masters are interested in ceremonies, in hierarchies and in giving names to people in accordance with their different stations and capacities, like, for example, the Sanusi spiritual masters of Libya who spiritually, socially, politically and economically led and ruled a very large network of villages and towns for nearly a century. On the other hand, some spiritual masters do not use a formal or ceremonial form of initiation, either due to the nature of their position in society or because they do not consider it necessary. So the socio-cultural environment and the inherent nature of the spiritual masters themselves are two major factors which determine the degree of formality in any particular Sufi Order.

The ultimate aim of the Sufi master is to assist his close follower to discover Truth within the self and to be enlightened about reality. In order to be fulfilled at all times, it is important to discover the causes of unhappiness. The essential cause of all dissatisfaction is rooted in the transgression of limits, waywardness, desires, expectations, fears, anxieties and other aspects like lack of understanding of the nature of Reality. From the Sufi point of view, the basic acts of worship which are defined by the Islamic Law, such as the ritual prayer, fasting in the month of Ramadan, the alms tax, the pilgrimage to Mecca and so on, are, although necessary, not sufficient for most of the people who are sick in this vast hospital called the world. The globe is God's hospital, and the Messengers, the Prophets and the saints or spiritual masters are the physicians of the soul. Since there are different kinds of illness, there are different wards in the hospital. There are clinics where the patients do not stay for very long; there are wards where the patients stay for several weeks or months; and there is a surgical ward where the physician, or Sufi master, is constantly engaged in 'operating' on his patients. We also find that the 'medicines' are prescribed in accordance with the specific requirements of the patient, taking the total environment and all the surrounding circumstances into consideration.

The ultimate function of a Sufi master is to move the seeker gradually, according to his pace, to a level at which he is able to read the primal 'book' that is within his 'heart'. If the seeker learns this art and becomes strong and acts at will, then obviously he is progressing and evolving. The spiritual master's objective is to part with and transmit to others what he has himself already attained. This process, as stated earlier, can be enhanced when the environment as well as the companionship is right, and when the close follower has the intention to learn and the will to act, and acts appropriately. The teacher can do little if the seeker or the close follower does not want to advance. The traveller can give up at any stage of the journey, even when there is only one step left. However, at times, even if the close follower wants to advance, it is not guaranteed that his objective will be fulfilled according to expectations. Shaykh al-Fayturi (d. 1979) says the following about the dilemma of the teacher in one of his odes:

No matter how much the teacher strives,
No matter how much the close follower wants,
No matter how sincere he is, spending days and nights
[in worship],
Ultimately enlightenment is a gift from Allah.

The teacher's function is to guide the seeker along a disciplined path to the point at which he is able to sit in absolute watchfulness without watching anything. This is the pure, simple, ultimate height of the meditative condition. It is just to be. From there on, it is only Allah Who can help. So the seeker has to complete half the circle himself, but the other half is not in his hands. You go as high as you can climb, and then let go!

According to the experience of the Sufis, the rate of progress along the spiritual path is not linear. In mechanistic studies, such as learning a language, progress is fairly linear. The more time one spends practising the language, the more one will be proficient in it, because it is something which is programmable and therefore quantifiable, and therefore easier to acquire. The inner sciences, on the other hand, are all qualifiable but difficult to quantify. If one could die completely to all attachments right now, then awakening would immediately be attained. Otherwise one has to go through the drudgery of discipline, constant reminding and constant affliction in order to arrive at complete awareness. Spiritual progress is not measured in the same way that one measures other endeavours. One may spend years without anything noticeable happening, and then suddenly in two days everything happens. One may spend years obeying one's teacher, and feeling that not much progress has been made, when in reality a great deal of spiritual 'rust' may have been removed during that period. It is like removing several inches of rust, and still not being able to discern the metal base beneath it, when in fact the metal may be only under just one more millimetre of rust. We are not able to measure spiritual progress externally, for it is based on the purity of the 'heart' and the willingness to abandon attachments. It depends upon the degree of the seeker's submission to the Divine. At first one submits by using one's reasoning and intellect and by learning all the causal relationships. Later on, spiritual progress takes on its own momentum. Then, simple submission leads to sweeter and more spontaneous submission without any questioning. Until this state is reached, nothing much can happen. Thus the time that it takes for certain openings to occur is not that easily measurable. A proper relationship between seeker and spiritual master is necessary to enable continuous progress. The Sufi master Imam Junayd's closest follower was called Shibli, and Imam Junayd (d. 910) loved him dearly. Once, during a gathering, one of its members started admiring and praising Shibli in his and the others' presence. Imam Junayd interrupted and started recounting Shibli's faults and shortcomings. Shibli was embarrassed and quietly dragged himself away from the gathering. When he had gone, Imam Junayd said, 'I protected him with the shield of insult from the poisonous arrows of flattery.' This was because Imam Junayd knew that Shibli was about to reach a spiritual station, and that if the praises had not been curtailed, they would have inflated his ego and created a barrier. The greatest barrier to inner awakening is having an opinion about oneself.

The whole Sufi way of life is about giving up attachments, and the greatest and the worst attachment happens to be knowledge. There is an anecdote about Imam Abu Hamid al-Ghazzali (d. 1111) in this context. When Imam al-Ghazzali left Baghdad in order to search for Sufi masters, he had acquired all the outer knowledge of the Islamic sciences, but his innermost was not yet awake. He took with him two mules loaded with books. On the way he was stopped by a robber who wanted to take all his books. Imam al-Ghazzali offered him everything except the books, but the robber only wanted the books, and took them. Seven or eight years later, when Imam al-Ghazzali had fulfilled his Sufi quest, a man appeared before him in Mecca. Apparently it was the Prophet al-Khidr, who is called Elijah in the Judaic tradition, who informed Imam al-Ghazzali that if it had not been for the theft of his books, he would have remained the slave of those books and would not have discovered the real 'Book' of knowledge that is within everyone's heart. Imam Ali says in this context, 'You are the evident [original] "Book".'

Books are needed initially as an aid to inner discovery, but when a person grows stronger with inner knowledge, he needs less external aids. Books are like the push-chair which a child only needs at the beginning of its life. Unfortunately, however, many so-called scholars keep their push-chairs for the rest of their lives. On the other hand, many pseudo-sufis tend to dismiss not only books but also recitations as altogether unnecessary. This simplistic attitude is nothing other than a form of self-elevation, which is a perversion of and a digression from the real spiritual path. Books and recitations are essential aids in assisting inner awakening, and can neither be totally relied on nor totally ignored.

The seeker of knowledge and gnosis has to follow the path under the guidance of a teacher until there comes a point when he has to be left alone. The teacher is like a crutch, on which the seeker no longer has to rely once he can walk. The time comes when the close follower no longer needs a physical master as he is now plugged directly into the original power source. If someone says that he needs an outer teacher all his life, then he has falsely limited the true extent of human potential and divine mercy and generosity. If someone says that he does not need a master at all, then he is arrogant and conceited and will live under the tyranny of the lower self.

However, for every rule there is an exception. There is an exception in the case of those people who do not need an outer master, or who do not appear to have a visible, physical master to direct and guide them. In the Sufi tradition, such people are called Uwaysis. This term is derived from the name of a man who was called Uways al-Qarani, and who lived in Yemen in the time of the Prophet Muhammad. Although he had not met the blessed Prophet physically, he had seen him in his visions. It is said that the blessed Prophet mentioned this great saint by saying, 'The breath of the Merciful comes to me from Yemen.' When people learned of his spiritual rank, Uways tried to hide behind the ordinariness of being a herder of camels and sheep, and seclusion became his way of life. When he was questioned about this, he would say, 'Making supplication for people in their absence is better than visiting them, for aspects of their egos, such as their dress or self-image, may distract my attention.' He also used to say, 'Enjoining good did not leave me with one friend,' and 'I asked every hungry man to forgive me, for I have nothing in this creation except whatever is in my stomach.' Uways became, for the later Sufis, the prototype of the inspired Sufi who does not identify himself with any particular Sufi Order. Such Sufis receive their initiation or their light directly from the Prophet's light, without the physical presence and guidance of any living spiritual master.

A few pseudo-sufis who do not follow, nor wish to follow, any genuine spiritual master to guide them on the spiritual path, exploit the situation and falsely call themselves Uwaysis. This is one of the tricks and deceptions of the lower self which does not wish to be groomed or to submit to Allah. Real genuine Uwaysis are rare. People genuinely interested in Sufism follow a path of self-improvement, self-awareness and self-awakening, by following the guidance provided by the Sufi master at hand.

6 · PSEUDO—SUFISM

Basically speaking, what we mean by the term pseudo-sufism is an incomplete path. It is an incomplete teaching which is not enough to guide the seeker all the way along the spiritual path which leads to self-knowledge and gnosis of Allah. Every religion and prophet, whether genuine or false, advocates moral virtues such as generosity, goodness, kindness, love and so on. However these qualities cannot take root and grow without being protected by a 'container' of outer laws and beneficial behaviour. We find that every society or culture advocates its version of what is considered good and virtuous, but these qualities cannot develop and bear fruit unless they are protected and guarded by the outer bounds of laws which enable them to be nourished and to grow continuously and purposefully. More specifically, as regards the spiritual path and the teacher and the taught, we find that the pseudo-sufi leaders do not possess all the attributes of a true spiritual master, which have already been mentioned, especially the express permission to teach and guide others on the path of self-knowledge, given by another enlightened and experienced teacher who himself has been given permission to teach, and so on, back to the Prophet Muhammad.

In recent times there has been a proliferation of so many gurus and mystical teachers. A large amount of literature has also appeared on Sufism and other spiritual paths, all of which allude to different techniques and the different methods used by Sufis to enhance self-awareness, enlightenment, centrality, contentment and the understanding of life. Some people who are searching for contentment and understanding of life go about it by experimenting with many different techniques given by random gurus, self-proclaimed masters and books. Such a situation can be compared to a sick person going to a pharmacy and picking up a few bottles of remedies, tonics and vitamins as the labels appeal to him. This action will surely benefit him to a certain extent, but it will not bring him, or restore him, to full health. To obtain and maintain health one needs to have sufficient knowledge about dietary balance, hygiene, exercise, rest and so on. In cases of severe imbalance and illness one will need the assistance of a physician. If a person is not taught the outer law and adherence to it, together with inner disciplines and practices, by an accomplished teacher, then he will not travel very far along the path of knowledge. Random experimentation will not result in the ultimate steady state of balanced inner health and awakening.

Many Knights Templars who travelled with the crusaders to the Muslim lands were influenced by the Sufi practices which they encountered, and adopted and adapted them. Some Christian gnostics also found Sufi practices, such as invocation of Allah followed by contemplation and reflection, to be beneficial. These Sufi practices, when taken out of context and confused, led to freemasonry and other secret societies. Some of their members ended up as rulers, or king-makers, or in other positions of influence and power. In such a type of distorted Sufism, ritual is mistaken for reality, and form for essence. However, some of these distorted practices do bestow some powers and advantages on their practitioners, albeit minor and erratic ones.

Another form of pseudo-sufism, which has become active and popular in our times, is indulgence in intellectual pleasure through the study of Sufi literature and Sufi Orders. During the last 150 years, much research into Sufism has been undertaken, both in the West and in the East, by orientalists and Muslims alike. This is like compiling menus on Sufism rather than actually partaking in the feast. They discuss and analyse which Sufi menu, that is which Sufi Order, seems to be better, but without tasting any of them. How can you evaluate something which you have not experienced? Intellectual discussion about Sufism cannot lead to inner awakening and enlightenment, because Sufism is a feast which can only be consumed.

In pseudo-sufi movements we find much euphoria and temporary states of excitement which are achieved by utilising certain practices and techniques. Occasionally they bring about a state of upliftment and delight. However such states are not lasting and are the result of a combination of several variable factors. The true art of Sufism leads the seeker towards the steady state of being contented, integrated, wise, courteous, kindly and at peace. To occasionally feel inner delight and contentment is not difficult to achieve, but in order to reach a station which is lasting, one needs to adhere to the primal way that is intended by the original way of Islam, with its outer laws, code of conduct and integrated way of life. Although inner development is possible to a certain degree without following the outer laws, if a person wishes to develop himself fully, then he has to participate in the Islamic Law and way of life fully.

7 · SUFI PRACTICES

The outer practices of the Sufis include varying amounts of prayers, invocations, recitations and supplications. If a Sufi Order developed in a nomadic environment, then we find most of their practices being performed while the caravan is on the move, and with many of the gatherings and circles of remembrance of God occurring at the beginning or the end of the night, because the caravan is stationary at these times. If a Sufi Order became active amidst the people of the bazaar in a city such as Qum, for example, or Fes, then we find a different pattern of practices, in which gatherings tend to take place in the afternoon or early evening or at a time which is convenient for shopkeepers.

We often find that not only the local ecology and physical environment had a lot to do with the type of Sufi practices which predominated in a certain area, but also the culture, class and socio-economic conditions of the group which played the most prominent role in these practices. We find that some Sufi Orders became almost exclusively for the well-off and the influential in society. For example, the Tijani Order in North Africa seems to have attracted those who were politically powerful, whereas the Darqawi Order has been predominantly followed by the poor. Sometimes a Sufi Order which used to generally attract the poor has

44

changed and started to attract the wealthy and powerful people, perhaps because of the arrival of a new spiritual master, or other significant changes in circumstances.

The outer climatic and weather conditions also influence the outward form of Sufi practices. We find that the members of the Sufi Orders which are in the deserts often sit or stand in rows for their practices. However, in the mountains or in places where it is necessary to be indoors and more confined, we find them sitting in concentric circles for their practices. There is nothing sacrosanct about these ways. It is the intuitive heart of the teacher which discovers the appropriate method to bring his 'patients' to health. When a certain specific Sufi practice or system is transplanted or transported from one environment to another, then it sometimes becomes anomalous, because that practice or system is only really suited for a particular environment and time, or for a particular kind of people. For example, the practice of remembrance of God by invocation, recitation and chanting is often done very vigorously and loudly by robust peoples like the Kurds, or the people of the Atlas mountains in North Africa, whereas among the city dwellers who are less physically strong, and who have a softer lifestyle, we find a far milder style of chanting and invocation. It is more musical, and can often end up becoming decadent and degenerating to the use of musical instruments.

Thus the outward forms of Sufi practices depend upon the environment, the time, the place, the ecology and the economic situation and social fibre of the people who belong to the Sufi Order. Despite all the variations that appear in different conditions, one thing which we find that all genuine Sufis have in common is that their practices result in outer discipline and inner openings and delights. They remind the sincere seeker and the close follower that the main purpose of life is to awaken, to learn the art of abandonment and submission, and to discover the unitive power behind everything. They bring people together on a common basis, since many of the spiritual practices are socially related such as weekly or monthly gatherings, while enabling each individual within the gathering to arrive at his own particular understanding of reality.

A good analogy that we can give of the Sufi Orders and their various styles and types of practice is that of cuisine. The menu of the cuisine of Canton in China, for example, is very different to that of Prague in Czechoslovakia or of Omdurman in Sudan. However, a meal is a meal, and if it is prepared with the correct ingredients, with attention and love, then it produces nourishment and well-being. Only its taste and its ingredients differ from place to place, but the purpose behind all food is the same.

The prominent characteristic of a Sufi Order is that the menu is appropriate to the season, climate and environment, just as ethnic foods are produced according to the climate and ecology of the land in which they occur. Some Sufi practices are far more rigorous than other. Some Sufis engage in their practices and night vigils in a sitting position. Some perform them standing, some reclining, and others adopt various different postures. Some use visual aids, and others do not. Each Sufi Order has developed its appropriate technique to scale the mountain of the self. The aim of a Sufi is to reach the pinnacle of his self, overcome the barriers of mind and intellect and become spontaneously aware of beingness. So the spiritual wayfarer is like a mountaineer. When a skilled mountaineer reaches the summit of the mountain peak, he becomes qualified to guide the novices further down the mountain on how to throw the rope and climb on.

The meditation practices and night vigils of the Sufis differ according to the place, time and particular orientation of the spiritual master. Some spiritual masters are far more ecstatic than others. Some are more serious or sober in their outer manner. However, all of them have something in common, just as master chefs in a kitchen have the love of food and knowledge of cooking in common. The spiritual masters share a state of inner silence and contentment. According to them, since the creation began from silence, anyone who wishes to start living must return to that point or origin – utter silence – an inner silence in which there is no vision, no memory, no thought, no movement.

In order to attain inner silence, the first requirement is to achieve outer or physical silence, which requires a healthy body. This is why many of the Sufi masters also practise medicine in order to be able to treat themselves and their close followers. For if the body is twitching all the time, how can one sit still? The outer, that is the physical body, is required to be still so as to facilitate inner stillness. So many of the Sufi masters have been practitioners of healing. The prophets were physicians of the outer as well as of the inner. They were masters of unity, of unifying the inner and the outer. They were unitarians. The goal of the Sufi is to scale higher and higher in consciousness and to reach the pinnacle of awakening, at which point he sees that the inner and the outer are perfectly unified.

THE MEANING OF THE
OUTER LAW AND THE INNER REALITY
(*SHARI'AH* and *HAQIQAH*)

According to the Sufis, everything we witness in this creation has a measure of polarity in it. Also, every phenomenon in creation is cyclical. A phenomenon is seen as if it starts from one point and ends in another and both the points meet. For example, the story of creation begins with the hydrological cycle. Water from the ocean evaporates, becomes cloud and then it rains and runs back to the sea. The same principle can be applied to the outer law and the inner reality. The Arabic word for the outer law is *shari'ah* which means a road or a way. When one embarks on it, it is like putting a canoe into the river in order to reach the ocean. If the traveller has a unific vision, if he is a man of unity, then he will recognise that although it is a river, it has a direction which will lead to its original nature and reality, which is that of the ocean. The Arabic word for the inner reality is *haqiqah* which means the truth. The ocean is the inner reality and the river is the outer road. The river would have no purpose or meaning if it was not to end at the ocean, and yet its origin is from the ocean!

As regards the people of vision and insight, of genuine connectedness and unity, the moment they step into the outer law, they perceive that they have stepped into the inner reality. From the Sufi point of view, if a person is seeking the depth of meaning and transformation in his life, then the moment he takes on the outer law, he at once realises its inner meaning and spirit. For example, the outer law obliges a person to perform outer purification, which is a combination of ritually washing the whole body in certain circumstances, and ritually washing only certain parts of the body in others, before doing the prayer. Now if a person has a unific vision of life and is after the knowledge of unity, then he will realise that this knowledge cannot be attained unless he is both outwardly and inwardly purified, and he will extend that requirement of the outer law. He will purify his skin and flesh, not only by ritual washing, but also by being watchful about eating and drinking the right type of foods and beverages. Beyond that, he will purify his heart, his intentions and his thoughts. This is the unific view of the outer law, or code of conduct. It simply and directly leads to the inner reality.

The outer Islamic Law, as we mentioned earlier, is the complete and final law of God revealed to the blessed Prophet Muhammad. It is based on the laws of conduct that were revealed directly in the Qur'an, and on the ways and teachings of Muhammad. These laws make it possible for every member of society to go deeper inwardly and to evolve towards the higher consciousness which is the intention and purpose behind this creation. Inner development, which is the aim of Sufism, is not possible without exoteric Islam. Esoteric interest will not be sufficient unless a person has the protection of the outer bounds of the outer code of conduct. Water cannot be contained without a container, nor an egg yolk without a hard shell. In the same way, the outer law is like a shell which protects the inner reality, like the exterior insulation that protects the inner core which safely carries what would otherwise be very volatile energy.

Now where does the outer law end and the inner reality begin? One is to do with the outer and the gross, and the other with the inner and the subtle. It is like saying that this is the river and there is the ocean, when in fact they are both aspects of one system interconnected by one reality, which is water.

From the Sufi point of view, man needs to embrace and submit to both the outer law and the inner reality, because he encompasses both. The human being is an isthmus, or interspace, between the two. He is involved in the outer law, or code of behaviour, in the sense that he is a physical, material entity, and he is involved in the inner reality in the sense that there is something within him which is beyond time and space. So inwardly, he is inner reality, and outwardly, he is outer law. The great Sufi masters say:

> Whoever has the outer law without the inner reality
> has left the right way;
> Whoever has the inner reality without the outer law
> is a heretic;
> Whoever unites the two of them has realisation.

The outer Islamic Law is a divinely revealed law. In nature there are certain laws which one cannot transgress or break. However within their boundaries, man can bring about some changes. Take for example a household in which the overall rules of the house are fixed, but within which rules one allows the child to do quite a lot of things as it pleases in one particular room. The child can for example, rearrange the furniture or put certain objects on the wall and so on. However as far as the style of the furniture or the actual boundary of the room are concerned, the child has no say or choice. Naturally, some bounds or rules are flexible, but there is always a final limit. The knowledge of these limits and the appropriate behaviour which is necessary to remain within them is the concern of the outer Islamic Law. To respect and love this outer law is to respect and love our natural, physical reality.

All of the prophets and messengers attained an exceptional quality of unveiling of some of the divine laws, both those which govern existence and those by which they are governed in existence, according to the circumstances, place and time in which they lived. They all reinforced each other. None of the prophets or messengers denounced his predecessors. If there was any abrogation of previous laws, then this was because the earlier human reality or consciousness was still evolving and was not yet ready for what was to come. For example, look at the drinking of alcohol. In a hot desert climate, it was not possible to store fruit for long without it fermenting, and so thousands of years ago, wine was a natural result of the long fruit season. People were permitted to drink this wine though its purpose was not to become intoxicated. Then a time came when it became possible to brew chemically-produced alcohol on a large scale, so that man was capable of seriously damaging both himself and his ecology by the intake of alcohol. Accordingly the final revealed law of Islam warns against this and prohibits the consumption of alcoholic drinks, even in moderation, altogether.

So there is always a sequence and a purpose behind the abrogation of certain divine laws, which were revealed to an earlier prophet, by a later prophet. All the prophets were in *islam*, that is in submission, in the sense that each one had surrendered their self to God, and the outer law, or code of conduct, which each one brought was a confirmation and continuation of that brought by his predecessor, of one complementary divine law. It is like building a city in different phases, in different times. As the city is built, certain rules and regulations become clear, until the entire city is completed. Then all the rules and regulations that have evolved and become necessary in the course of construction are unified and completed, all in accordance with the original master plan!

The Prophet Moses revealed many laws which are totally in line with what came before him and what came after him. Over a period of centuries, however, these laws were tampered with, and only the letter of the law remained important. So the Prophet Jesus appeared, and breathed the spirit of the law back into them, without changing the laws of Moses as such. He questioned the manner in which these laws were being applied, and sought to redress the imbalance between the spirit and the letter of the law, by emphasising the qualities of courteous behaviour, gentleness, faith, trust and all the other moral Christian values. Later, the Prophet Muhammad confirmed the same original laws in a fully balanced way and in a language and a culture which were different to those of the earlier prophets. The Prophet Muhammad abrogated some laws and, as divinely instructed, brought some new laws, thereby completing the code of behaviour of the prophetic path.

The prophetic laws are divinely revealed codes of behaviour brought by individuals who were exceptionally sensitive in their connectedness between the worlds of the seen and the unseen. Their 'hearts' were like mirrors that reflected the intended original laws in the unseen and in the more tangible form which they gave to humanity. These laws are not rigid or repressive, and within them there is a great deal of freedom to create new and more detailed by-laws and rules to organise human society. For example, the exact amount of food allowed for daily human consumption has not been divinely revealed. On the other hand, it is a natural and commonly understandable law that if a person does not eat for long enough, he will die. However, it is not as easily understandable, for example, that if homosexuality becomes prevalent, then society could perish. This is because we have not yet lived in an environment where homosexuality has completely prevailed. So the divine law clearly forbids the practice of homosexuality, since otherwise society could be destroyed and recycled. Naked nature will come to its aid, and the examples of Sodom and Gomorrah will repeat themselves. Then there are subtler laws which deal with less obvious transgressions, such as usury. It has been revealed to many prophets and messengers, and especially emphasised to the last great ones – Moses, Jesus and Muhammad – that usury will cause the destruction of any society that indulges in it. Jesus denounced the practice of usury, and many Jews rejected him because he threatened to destroy their abusive habit, on which they depended for their livelihood. Today we see virtually the whole world possessed, obsessed and controlled by the system of usury which operates by means of the legalised banking systems.

The outer Islamic Law, as stated earlier, is the culmination of all the earlier revealed laws. Societies and cultures which follow the original divine laws will endure. An individual or society will benefit according to the extent to which these laws are applied. If a society or a country acts in generosity towards the poor and the needy, which is in accordance with all the divinely revealed laws, then as a result of this act, much good will come to those who are charitable. So whenever, inadvertently or advertently, an individual or a society performs good deeds, that act is in line with the Islamic Law. The longevity and well-being of a culture or a society depend on how close its practices are to the original outer Islamic Law. Since the majority of the Muslims today are not fully applying the Islamic Law, other than superficially, they too individually and collectively are being afflicted and punished by their own ignorance or wrongdoing.

In the history of human progress, we find that the revealed outer laws were very simple at the outset. However, as man's culture, civilisation and consciousness developed, the outer laws became more detailed and complex. People in early times had simple, primal ways and notions about life. Even today, some nomadic tribes have codes of conduct that are simply connected to man's innate nature. These codes are primal and very simple and straightforward. The leader of such a tribe generally possesses the most desirable qualities among his people. He is generous, strong, benign, selfless, compassionate and so on. These tribes continue with their lives for some time until suddenly an unworthy leader emerges, or the system is challenged by a more complex or advanced culture, and then their simple way of life is lost.

To summarise, the outer divine laws have been revealed in different formats over a period of time according to the needs of the age, and this process was completed in its totality 1,400 years ago. This master plan from the unseen, from the source of all creational realities, is part of its love and mercy upon people so that we are not left without guidance. The prophets and messengers revealed what was essential and necessary for the human condition. The laws and blueprints which they brought culminated in the final blueprint which is the Muhammadan code. Thus these various codes of outer laws are complementary and are readings from the same book. It is like the reading of different chapters from the same book or tablet. And within the parameters of the divinely revealed outer laws, there is room for man-made laws which are in harmony with them. The outer Islamic Law, as we have mentioned earlier, provides the body of the law, but within it the specifics – for example, how much tax should be levied upon the population for certain imported items – are left to the government of the day to decide. If the government needs a certain amount of money for a particular project, and people are wealthy, then an Islamic government can establish its own rules in order to collect this money by means of an extra tax, even though it is not expressly obligatory according to the Islamic Law. So there is great scope within the Islamic Law to prescribe rules and regulations which are appropriate to present circumstances and which are compatible with it. It is this flexibility, based on and within a precise form, which ensures that the outer law is indeed a means to the inner reality, and not an obstacle that covers it up or prevents access to it.

THE MEANING OF INNATE NATURE (*Fitra*)

According to the Qur'an, the creation began with the divine command, 'Be!' (Qur'an 16.40; 19.35; 36.82). Within that command is contained the entire book of Reality. From the Sufi point of view, every 'heart' contains a blueprint of truth. Most people know what happiness and unhappiness are, what contentment and discontentment are. How do they know this? How do I know that I am not content? How do I know that I am now disturbed? My body may be completely out of balance, and yet I will still know what balance and tranquillity are, and what discord and imbalance are. There is something within the core of everyone which reveals the truth. That something does not change, for it is primal and sub-genetic. Physically, everyone appears to be different, but that which is ingrained sub-genetically in man is his innate nature, as we mentioned earlier. The word in Arabic for innate nature is *Fitra*. The original blueprint of divine laws is preserved in this innate nature of man. If that blueprint is not tarnished or obscured, then it is easier for a man to recognise and acknowledge the messengers and Reality. In other words, if a person is brought up in a clean, natural and healthy environment, then his chance of discovering the truth and the way to freedom is better than that of others who are caught up within adverse environmental, racial or cultural constraints.

The Sufis always say that if you follow your 'heart', you will be all right. Allah also says in the Qur'an that the 'heart' never lies. How does one distinguish between guidance coming from the 'heart', and that which is coming from one's emotions, desires, fears and imagination? How does one distinguish one's original innate nature from one's imagination? The innate nature in each one of us has been tarnished to varying degrees, due to family and other influences during our early life. In order to return to our original state of innate nature, we need again the guidance of the outer code of divine law. This is why original Islam is much more easily followed by people who have not been educated or trained to analyse, doubt and debate.

In olden times, in China, India and the Middle East, we find that there were many prophets and saints. They all reflected the primal truth, which is that we have come from one Reality and our physical existence is not a permanent reality but only a shadow which we have to learn to transcend and, by so doing, discover within us that which is timeless and permanent. The early simple folk of tribes and villages in olden times could more easily reflect the ultimate truth behind creation. The great Sufi master, Ibn Arabi, says that the first group of people who will be admitted to the Garden of Paradise after death will be the simple folk.

Our innate nature is something with which every human being is endowed. It is like a spring of fresh, clear, cool water, or a well of sweet water. During a person's upbringing, however, and because of the intellectual clutter and culture which is gradually accumulated, the well begins to fill up with rubbish, and the time comes when it is found that there is no more fresh water flowing, because the well of his innate nature has been filled with debris. Many of those who live in crowded modern cities or in urban, industrialised societies have to do a lot of digging and archaeological work before reaching the original foundation and the source of the spring in the well.

These people need more discipline and hard work, such as meditation, reflection and intellectual de-brainwashing, than people who live in simple rural settings open to nature where material needs and competition are less, and whose innate nature is preserved so that part of the original blueprint of divine laws is still readable.

The difference between the wise simple folk who still have access to their innate nature and the prophets is that the latter receive the divine teaching through revealed ways, whereas the former receive understanding through witnessing, reflection and insight. Many others also are endowed with inspiration whenever there is a crack in their veil, the veil being nothing other than the lower self, and once it is removed, there are strange and wondrous glimpses of reality.

We have seen that Islam, the original divinely intended way of conduct which, if adhered to, leads a person towards his Creator, is not a religion that came into existence some 1,400 years ago, but rather, is the Adamic way, moulded on the first creation from the beginning of humanity. With the rise of Adamic consciousness, there arose parallel to it an inner crack, or innate knowledge or understanding, regarding how to behave in this existence so as to avoid being confused.

The way of Islam is the Adamic way of behaviour. Every prophet, every man of awakening and freedom, has been in submission and is therefore a Muslim. Every thinker, philosopher and wise man has been a Muslim to varying degrees of clarity and consciousness. All human beings in fact are born in submission to natural reality and therefore in Islam. It is the society and the parents who often then corrupt that innate Islamic state. There are people all over the world who discover Islam in themselves during some period of their lives, and not as a result of having come across the conventional religion of Islam. Rather, it is an echo of something far deeper and pre-creational which is centred in the hearts of all human beings. However the conventions, both behavioural and conceptual, which society, community and personal habit impose upon a person, veil recognition of this reality. Hence we need divine laws to guide us to lead a life which is unified and which leads to knowledge of unity.

Original Islam has existed right from the beginning of humanity and it was revealed in different degrees until the totality of it was revealed through the Prophet Muhammad in such a way that Allah promised to people that it would be preserved forever. Accordingly, no one has any excuse if they try to distort or change it. The differences that exist between the various Muslim schools of law on matters of Islamic Law are minor and insignificant. However if people want to see differences, then they see great differences, and this often happens to those who do not have access to their innate nature.

THE PURPOSE OF SUFI PRACTICES

The chief purpose of Sufi practices is the restoration of wholeness in people. The Sufi masters, therefore, prescribe different medicine to their followers in the form of different kinds of practices with different intensities according to the type of illness which is being treated. We find that every Sufi Order has its own particular invocation, its own chanting and recitation, and its own ceremonies and methods of sitting or standing. As well as the practices which are done collectively, the Sufi teacher often prescribes specific remedies for particular individuals, for example, if one of his close followers is ill or needs specific treatment, such as intense periods of night vigils or watchfulness. Whatever their apparent differences, one element which we find in common in all of the Sufi Orders is a deep relationship between the spiritual master and the close follower. The relationship is based on trust, love and obedience to the master. It is said that the best follower for a master is like a rag in the hands of a washerman. It is through such submissiveness and obedience that the meaning of the teaching of the spiritual master is quickly absorbed.

We also find in many circles that out of love and respect for their teachers, the followers even emulate the outer habits and garb of their teachers. Sometimes, however, this copying is carried to such an extreme that it loses all meaning and becomes an empty outer imitation, which is of no benefit, rather than being a sign of union by being similar.

An example of this extreme imitation is seen in the case of a teacher who, because of the poor condition of his teeth, always ate his food noisily. His close followers, without ever inquiring into the reason for this habit, foolishly imitated him. Imam Jafar as-Sadiq never used a toothstick to clean his teeth during the last years of his life. Some of his followers thought that he had come up with a new way of keeping his teeth clean without using a toothstick, even though this was a habit which was dear to the Prophet Muhammad, and which all his followers like to emulate. Imam Jafar told them that his teeth were so weakened that if he used a toothstick, it would cause further damage. What is important is the relationship between the spiritual master and the close follower, due to which the follower's state is lifted towards the state of the master.

The major concern of a Sufi is to be detached from that which is transitory and which distracts a person from spiritual progress. In order for one to stop being distracted constantly by the mundane aspects of life, one needs a way to deflect the mind from thinking about such matters. Different invocations, as well as single-pointed attention directed towards a particular divine name or attribute, or other appropriate forms of remembrance of God, all narrow the thought process and channel the energies. Obviously, repeating a specific sound helps towards achieving single-pointedness. It is the practice of single-pointedness that enables a person to be less distracted. Single-pointedness is such a desirable state for human beings that we find many recreational activities, hobbies, sports, and indeed all scientific and investigative endeavours, centred around it. By following a golf ball, one is less distracted by other events around and there is therefore less clutter and noise in the mind.

In the same way, when a Sufi repeats *La ilaha illa'llah*, which means *There is no god but Allah*, for a while, then his thoughts are gradually wiped away. His mind computer is cleared. The human mind is ideally suited when called upon to deal with matters of a natural, causal or existential nature. It is most conducive to rational or logical thinking and needs to be free of excessive psychological or emotional considerations, which tend to bog it down. So the purpose of remembrance of Allah is to de-psychologise the mind. It is to de-brainwash it and clean its filters. There are different forms of remembrance of Allah for different illnesses in different people in different circumstances, different times and different conditions.

As a means to arriving at single-pointedness, invoking the divine attributes is important. Attributes like the Compassionate (ar-Rahman), the Patient (as-Sabur), the Creator (al-Khaliq), the Provider (ar-Razaq), the All-Pervading (al-Latif), Love (al-Wadud), Peace (as-Salam), and so on, are repeatedly invoked and called upon, according to one's need and state. The word Allah which indicates the Essence of Reality is also frequently invoked. The two attributes, the Living the Eternal (al-Hayyu al-Qayyum), sound very similar to the Sanskrit invocation AUM when invoked together. There is no doubt that chanting these divine names and attributes helps a great deal in bringing about the desired states of centrality and tranquillity.

These practices and recitations help at all levels, but they are best administered by a spiritual master. Haphazardly picking up and repeating some invocations or Sufi practices which one has read or heard about may produce some beneficial effects, but not of lasting value. Furthermore, there is no substitute for the wisdom and knowledge and company of a true spiritual master.

There is a story about a curio collector who found an ancient manuscript written in Arabic. In it there was a recipe for a cure for all liver diseases. The instructions stated that a black snake should be ground up and mixed with various other ingredients. So the curio collector found a black snake, prepared the medicine, and waited for a wealthy person to be afflicted with liver problems. When a young prince contracted hepatitis, our self-appointed doctor rushed to the royal palace with his secret potion. Within a day, the prince was dead and the curio collector in jail for life. To the uninitiated, the words snake and seed in Arabic appear to be one and the same, for they are written almost identically except for a missing dot.

It is very important that the prescription comes from the right person. The true spiritual master, if he is good, genuine and in submission, will give his close follower a specific remedy in a specific fashion. It is like instructing someone about where to find buried treasure. Precise directions and the exact number of steps to be taken are imperative, otherwise an enthusiastic but discourteous seeker may decide to add a few steps of his own and miss the treasure altogether.

The same approach applies to following the instructions given by a spiritual master regarding different forms of remembrance of Allah, prayers and invocations. Occasionally, we find spiritual prescriptions being given by unqualified or superstitious persons with good intentions, but the results are ineffective or only temporary.

There is no doubt, however, that any meditation or divine adoration and invocation or recitation is spiritually helpful. It is like taking a general tonic which helps everyone, whatever their ailments may be. However in the case of acute or chronic illness, a tonic only brings temporary and limited relief, and the services of a skilled physician are required. The various forms of remembrance of Allah of every Sufi Order are helpful. Every recitation that has come from a genuine spiritual master does have some benefit, even for the one who recites them without having had them prescribed for him, but when a specific form of remembrance of Allah is individually prescribed by a spiritual master, and is transmitted from heart to heart, then an effective step towards freedom has been taken.

THE MEANING OF THE REMEMBRANCE OF ALLAH
(Dhikru'llah)

The Arabic word for remembrance is *dhikr*. Remembrance is of several types or levels. There is the remembrance of physical things which are in front of us, and there is the remembrance of one's desires, anxieties and so on. Along the spiritual path, remembrance relates to that which is in one's innate nature. It is the remembrance of the Essence of Allah the Almighty, of the Source of all manifestations and attributes. That source is within everybody. On the Sufi path, one is required to dis-remember everything else that is discernible, everything that is other than Allah, in order to return to the original remembrance. Allah. The Arabic word for remembrance of Allah is *dhikru'llah*.

So the original remembrance of Allah is already in every heart, whether one is aware of it or not. Through the guidance of a spiritual master, the seeker is led beyond, to a level where there is no remembrance of anything that is mentionable. Then that which has always been there, encompassing everything, is evidently experienced and witnessed. The purpose of Sufi practices is to be spontaneously aware of the absolute or central reality as well as remaining aware of the physical and material limitations of the phenomenal world which surrounds us. One is an inner awareness beyond the senses, and the other is an outer awareness which is based on the senses. So the aim of a Sufi teacher is to give the appropriate practices to his close follower and to watch over the results.

Generally speaking, about two hours are needed to obtain the benefits of remembrance of Allah. During the first half-hour, the meditator is primarily trying to quieten down his thoughts. In the next half-hour, he begins to enter the meditative state. During the third half-hour, generally speaking, there are no thoughts or mental visions, and meditation is established. During the last half-hour, real benefits begin to set in. Proper meditation begins when all awareness fades away and simple non-descript beingness sets in.

Any awareness during remembrance of Allah is a hindrance to entry into the realm of pure consciousness. Pure consciousness cannot be talked about. It must be experienced. It is the state of beingness.

Generally speaking, all mental processes are regarded as lower consciousness. All physical, material and causal aspects of life are in this category. Abstract thoughts and emotions are regarded as subtler and therefore higher. Within all human perceptions there are scales of consciousness. There are scales in our consciousness of hearing, seeing, understanding and so on. So consciousness is along a vertical scale. One can say the same thing about God's attributes. There are some attributes which have to do with the physical mechanisms that govern matter, all of which is permeated by divine order.

Physical consciousness relates to matter and mass, and is low on the scale of consciousness because it is gross. Higher on the scale is consciousness of mind, such as feelings, emotions and, for example, dislike of physical pain. Higher still is the intellectual consciousness of moral values, a sense of justice and equality, and so on.

The aim of a Sufi is to go higher than all intellectual consciousness. In the state of meditation, in the beginning, there is the consciousness of the physical body. Then the body is forgotten, but there is still the consciousness of ideas and thoughts. Through the technique of single-pointed meditation, all the ideas and thoughts are sublimated. Beyond that is the state of pure or highest consciousness where there is no consciousness of any discernible thing. It is an indescribable simple awareness. Now this is not the end of the meditation exercise. Actually, it signifies a new beginning. The end of all thoughts is the beginning of another dimension.

A simile of the process of meditation is that of sleep. When a person is going to sleep, he starts by turning down the covers and climbing into bed. He then prepares to relax and gradually becomes less conscious of his thoughts until physical consciousness ends altogether. The end of thought is the beginning of another form of consciousness which is called sleep. Sleep, like meditation, is subjective and experiential. It has to occur and is not talked about. The final stage in meditation is not describable for it is related to pure consciousness. Anything that is describable belongs to the realm of the physical world. The fact that one talks about an experience brings limitations to it. Once a person enters the zone of higher consciousness, he is not conscious of anything specific. The beginning of higher consciousness is the end of all other consciousness. Accordingly, description and talking about it also ends. It is an incredibly wonderful state, vast and timeless and non-dimensional. Bliss!

THE MEANING OF WATCHFULNESS (*Muraqabah*)

A very important Sufi practice is watchfulness. The Arabic word for watchfulness is *muraqabah*. It is practised in order to witness and sublimate one's own state. With the practice of watchfulness comes greater and greater sensitivity which results in the ability to witness the 'opening' within. Concentrated and advanced watchfulness occurs in retreat. During retreat, and when the real opening occurs, the seeker will recognise the vast emptiness and timelessness within himself. This is the culmination, so to speak, of self-awareness and self-watchfulness, and the beginning of what is considered as the process of gnostic awakening or enlightenment. All that this means is that the person is conscious at all times of the indescribable state within, which has no limits.

THE MEANING OF RETREAT (Khalwa)

We often come across the practice of retreat combined with other spiritual practices prescribed for forty days. Why forty days? In the natural world, there are numerous natural laws, many of which are cyclical. There are also many biological laws, such as those regulating reproduction and feeding, which follow a certain rhythm and time cycle. In the case of spiritual nourishment or rehabilitation, there are also optimum durations and frequencies.

In the tradition of Sufi seclusion practices, we often find a time of retreat being prescribed by the spiritual master for the close follower, usually for a period of forty days, or ten days, or seven or three days, and so on. For example, for the retreat period during the month of Ramadan, the Islamic month of fasting, it is required that one isolate oneself in the mosque in spiritual retreat for at least three days and usually for ten days.

The Sufi master places a seeker in retreat when he is fully prepared for it in body, mind and heart. The Arabic word for retreat is khalwa. Once in spiritual retreat, the purpose is, by means of remembrance of Allah and watchfulness, to leave all thoughts behind and through single-pointedness experience pure consciousness. During a close follower's retreat, his intake of food must be carefully regulated by the spiritual master. Equally, his mental, emotional and spiritual state is watched. Spiritual retreat and remembrance of Allah are of no use unless the seeker is ready to leave all aspects of creation behind him. One form of spiritual retreat is called a *chilla*, which means forty, and its duration is forty days. It is said that when a person is ready to be locked up for forty days, a breakthrough or opening may be achieved earlier, before the forty days have been completed.

The period of seclusion mentioned in the Qur'an relating to the Prophet Moses was a promise by God for forty days (Qur'an 2.51), thirty days to begin with and then an additional ten days (Qur'an 7.142). The Prophet Zachariah was instructed by God not to speak to people for three days (Qur'an 19.10). The Prophet Muhammad was asked, 'How many days should a person repent in order to be forgiven [awakened to reality]?' The Prophet replied, 'A year before death is sufficient.' Then immediately he said, 'A year is too long. A month before death is enough.' Then again he said, 'A month is too long.' He went on, progressively reducing the time period, until he said, 'An instant is enough.'

OTHER SUFI PRACTICES

Numerous Sufi masters and saints have come up with certain invocations, recitations, chants and supplications which help the seeker to purify and uplift himself. Circles and gatherings of remembrance of Allah are held to help purify the self by means of abandoning thought and concern with mundane affairs. Much help comes by concentrating on a special, specific sound repeatedly. The energy that emanates from the presence of many people in a circle of remembrance of Allah creates 'openings' to the 'heart' and produces light-heartedness in the seekers. Different spiritual masters, according to different circumstances and times, have brought about different remedies for curing the maladies of the self.

Some masters have found that the practice of the *hadra* is a useful method for enabling 'openings' to the 'heart'. The Arabic word *hadra* is usually defined as 'Sufi dancing' in this context, but literally it means presence, since those who do the *hadra* correctly are increased in their awareness of the ever-present, all-pervading presence of Allah. The *hadra*, which usually involves the invocation of the attribute of Allah the living *al-Hayyu*, can be done standing, chanting and swaying in groups. Some groups stand in circles, some of them stand in rows, and some sit in rows or circles, the men in one group, and the women in another separate group.

Some Sufis have taken some practices from Asia and Africa and innovated different ways and means of utilising them which are suitable for their particular needs. For example, some Sufis, particularly members of the Naqshbandi Order, use breathing exercises and intensive hyperventilation which increase the flow of oxygen into the bloodstream. These practices are quite similar to those performed by the yogis of India.

Some of these practices are open to the public, while others are meant only for the initiates and close seekers. Often they exclude children and very young people. In practically all cases, women and men are separated from each other, so that no disturbing energies cause any distraction.

The turning of the whirling dervishes is yet another curious practice. The principle behind it is that it is the outer form that can be left to roam and turn, while the inner centrality and its fixation remains still and is strengthened, just as the central core of a rapidly spinning top is completely still. Turning was mastered by Mawlana Jalal'ud-Din Rumi, who used to do it round a tree. In effect, he achieved single-pointedness by uniting two opposite realities – turning outwardly, stillness inwardly – in one being. During turning, the attention has to be directed inwards to the 'heart', and accordingly to Allah, for if it were directed outwards, the person turning would soon grow dizzy. Turning can bring about an ecstatic state if it is conducted under the proper supervision and guidance of a spiritual master.

The members of the Rifa'i Order display some spectacular and strange physical phenomena that cannot be easily explained. One such practice is piercing the body with a sword without there being any blood loss, and apparently without pain, which is performed while in a state of ecstasy. The perception and experiences of a person during a transformed state are very different to those which accompany normal consciousness.

Most of the Sufi Orders practise remembrance of Allah by chanting or singing, with the occasional use of musical instruments, especially drums. Music has entered into the practices of the Sufi Orders in a very limited way, and often for a temporary period under the guidance of a spiritual master. In the case of the Indian sub-Continent, the Sufis found that the Hindus were already very fond of music, so they also used music in order to bring them to the path of self-awareness, remembrance of Allah and joyful abandonment. So although musical instruments were used for that purpose and with that intention, they were however generally considered to be unnecessary distractions. Most of what is sung is concerned with the spiritual path and has no relationship to ordinary songs. They are often descriptions of how to liberate oneself from one's own shackles and how to be awakened.

So Sufi singing and dancing is part of the practice of shedding worldly anxieties and bringing about sensitivity within oneself by means of what is called *sama* which in Arabic means to hear. In the Sufi context this means anything to do with music or song that is intended for one's spiritual uplift and self-purification. All these practices have no significance other than to bring about a state of neutrality within oneself and the opening of the heart. They are not performed for the sake of entertainment as is the case with ordinary music which is rhythmic and exciting physically. The dance is for Allah, not for other people. We often find that whenever a real spiritual master is not present, music and singing get out of hand and lose their intended purpose. Music is a tool, and when left in the hands of those who know how to use it, it serves its intended purpose. Otherwise it can go out of control and cause damage.

THE IMPORTANCE OF TIME AND PLACE

Particular importance is attached to special places and times by spiritual masters for meditation, supplication and other spiritual practices. There are certain places which have natural qualities that are affected by, for example, the earth's electro-magnetic field and closeness to granite mountains or rivers and other sources of water. There are numerous places on this earth where people feel an affinity or a desire to be there. Also there are places which are repulsive, such as, for example, near high voltage electric power lines, which frighten away most animals who can feel the bad vibrations and who accordingly avoid such contamination, unlike most human beings who are not so sensitive.

Obviously, every place has a certain energy or eco-system. There are certain places on this earth which have a high energy concentration, such as Mecca, Medina, Jerusalem and the shrines of the earlier prophets and the great saints, spiritual masters and spiritual leaders, to which people are constantly drawn. When one visits these places, one feels that a great event once took place there, and this feeling is often helpful in healing the heart and raising one's spiritual level. These places help a great deal if a person is guided and prepared to uplift his state.

The same comments apply to time. There is an important if subtle relationship between time and the changing seasons, the phases of the moon, fluctuations in temperature and other time-related changing conditions. There is no doubt that there are tendencies and trends within the cosmic sphere with regard to positive and negative energies that affect both the physical as well as the spiritual climate on earth at specific times. For example, it is not known on what specific night during the Islamic month of the fast of *Ramadan* that the 'night of power' will occur, but tradition holds that it is either on the 21st or the 23rd or the 25th or the 27th or the 29th night of that particular lunar month. On this night, it is as if all the appropriate cosmic forces come into focus together and are magnified. On a night such as this, it seems as though there is no spiritual lid on the 'sky' and it is much more conducive to sit in meditation. Remembrance of Allah and night vigils at a time such as this, in a place like Mecca or Medina or the shrine of a great spiritual master, are more effective than at other times in other places.

So the knowledge of time and place is an important aid when following spiritual practices. For example it is said that the last third of the night, before dawn sets in, is one of the best times for remembrance of Allah and making supplications, and that the best place for such practices is somewhere which is clean and free of wrong actions. However, if a person is determined and well guided, then place and time is of less significance to him. When Imam Ali was asked, 'Which days of the year are ominous?', he replied, 'Do not be an enemy of days and no day will be your enemy.' From the elevated height of his spiritual station, he did not make a distinction or see a difference between good and bad days. He simply witnessed the divine mercy and love of Allah all the time wherever he was, even when he was in the act of being struck by an assassin's sword as he prostrated before the One Who is beyond time and place.

The enlightened master sees the entire cosmos in his heart. He regards his heart as the sacred house of worship of Allah at the centre of the cosmos. He sees Allah's trace at all times everywhere. However, for a lay person, in spiritual matters, it appears as if Allah is more present at certain times and in certain places than at other times or places.

The ultimate purpose of all genuine Sufi practices is the experiential awakening into the infinite realities as they unfold in their own natural way within each heart. The sparks of light that emanate from within are innumerable and infinite in their combination and permutation, engulfing all attributes, and yet their essence is one. The real Sufi will not rest until he is established in the knowledge of the essence, and when that occurs, all other lights, manifestations and glorious attributes fade in the effulgence of that inner awakening.

8 · SUFI STATES

STAGES OF AWAKENING

The first step for the seeker to achieve is witnessing, which is 'to be'. Witnessing has many levels. A child witnesses physical things that are proximate and close to him, such as his mother's face, his toys and so on. As one grows in maturity, one begins to witness an ever increasing display of natural phenomena, most of which are causal, as well as becoming aware of other laws that govern this existence. This witnessing expands wider and goes deeper as one grows in experience and wisdom.

The acute observer begins to witness the laws of duality everywhere. The Andalusian Sufi Ibn Arabi says that the entire existence is suspended between the opposites of what is praiseworthy and blameworthy, or desirable and undesirable. Everything in existence is either what one wants or what one rejects. We want health, and dislike illness. We want wealth, and despise poverty. We want freedom, and resist shackles. The entire creation is hinged upon opposites.

Subtler witnessing relates to the inner aspects of reality such as the self. The process of witnessing goes on until one ends up close to the inner core of unitive reality and pure consciousness. In the beginning one is conscious of duality, but as one's spiritual dimension grows, one begins to see creation from the unitary perspective. Thus witnessing takes place from two different perspectives. One is used to witness outer phenomena, and the other to witness inner phenomena. This witnessing goes on and on. In the beginning, a person is conscious of one thing or another, then he is conscious that he is conscious of this thing or the other, then he is generally conscious of his consciousness, which is a prelude to pure consciousness. No one can describe pure consciousness for it is beyond ordinary experience. It is for that reason that nobody can claim that he is in pure consciousness. The moment he talks, he has entered into an experiential state.

So witnessing is the first step towards self-knowledge. As regards self-knowledge, it is said that he who knows himself knows his Lord. However self-knowledge exists in many degrees. At an ordinary level, it relates to the lower self. To know how weak and dependent one is, is to recognise that one is seeking a Lord who is most mighty and self-sustaining. He who knows how selfish he is, can realise that he is seeking a Lord who is most generous. If he recognises his limitations, he may have a glimpse of the Limitless. In recognising how low one is, one may recognise how high Allah is. All this knowledge of the self is at a basic level. However, knowing oneself ultimately means knowing that the whole creation is encompassed within the self. Imam Ali says, 'You think that you are a small germ, but in you is encompassed the entire creation.'

So the first step for a seeker to take is to witness, pure and simple. It is to be watchful, to be aware, to allow that which is higher in you to enable you to witness what goes on within you. In the state of watchfulness, at the beginning, there is usually a storm of thoughts. With guidance and perseverance, these bubbles of thoughts surface and vanish. This is the stage of emptying out. It is the cleaning of the mind-processor so that no psychological or emotional memories remain to contaminate the mind-computer. Then begins the process of sweetening. In order to achieve the ability to connect with the inner central core of one's self at any time and in any place, one needs to be sweetened. It is a process of displacement. It is like a bucket of muddy water which becomes purified by placing it under a running tap of sweet, clean water, until all the mud in the water has been displaced, and the water in the bucket purified. The speed at which the tap flows depends on the size and capacity of the bucket. This is where a teacher is required for help. If the seeker is ready, the teacher simply pushes him into the ocean of awakening, which is what happened with Shaykh Abu Hasan ash-Shadhili. When he reached his teacher, after having already mastered all the outer knowledges of Islam, he was simply asked to renew his ritual purification through washing. His spiritual master, Shaykh Abd as-Salam ibn Mashish, told him to descend the mountain and renew his ritual purification through washing, and then to return. When Shaykh ash-Shadhili returned, it only took one look from his spiritual master for him to understand the meaning of all that had gone on before and after and the purpose of the meeting between the two of them. The seeker recognised the teacher and the teacher recognised the seeker instantaneously. However, there are those seekers who need continuous sweetening, encouragement and guidance before inward purification can occur.

So sweetening is a process which is followed by purification. In actual life these three processes – emptying out, sweetening and purification – are carried out and take place simultaneously. They are three dimensions of the same process as they reinforce each other, leading towards the desired end result. They all go hand in hand.

As we discovered earlier, there are several dimensions to witnessing and awakening. One witnesses duality and what is behind the veils of experiencing wakefulness, sleep, happiness, displeasure and so on. The one who witnesses understands the inner nature of events and the root of experiencing. Allah says, 'We have sent you as a witness.' (Qur'an 33.45–6). So the first step in the Sufi path is to witness. After a person has witnessed the unfathomable Reality, he cannot but give the good news. He gives the good news by his very existence, for that itself is the good news. As the Sufi saying goes, 'You exude what is within you.' If he has witnessed the truth he will sing the truth. He will give the good news of the truth that man's reality is beyond time, and space, that he is of a divine reality and is here temporarily for the training and cultivation of the self, in order to be able to face and understand the meaning of this life and the next stage, after the physical death of the body. The good news is the certainty within one's self that whatever experiences, good or bad, one undergoes in this world, it is all part of a process of purification and preparation for the heart.

Life experiences cannot be static. Lack of advancement is backwardness and not merely being stationary. If we do not progress spiritually, then we are decaying. The Arabic word for decay which is *fisq* means the bursting of a date from its skin before it is fully ripe. It has transgressed its programme for maturation and fulfilment. It is accordingly natural that all the prophets have warned that, in accordance with the prescribed spiritual path, if man does not follow the intention behind creation, then there will be nothing but destruction and misery here in this world. Mankind will never be satisfied or content. Mu'awiya, the first Muslim king, with all that he possessed – which was in his time the greatest wealth ever – died most miserably. To this day, nobody knows where he is buried, although it is believed that his grave is beneath what is now the site of a public wash-house in Damascus in Syria. Some historians say that among the relics which he collected was some hair of the Prophet Muhammad, and that at the time of his death he said, 'Put them in my mouth so that they may help me to attain salvation.' Superstition comes in all manner of forms and at all levels!

In the Qur'an Allah commands Muhammad – and by extension his close followers – to invite people to the truth of Reality. This can occur only if they themselves have fulfilled the other requirements according to Allah's natural way. The Sufi way of the prophetic path points towards inviting people to the feast of light within. The light within cannot be kindled unless the lamp which protects it has been purified and made suitable for its radiation. The mirror of the 'heart' will not reflect the Truth if it is covered with layers of dust which have been allowed to accumulate upon it either inadvertently or through carelessness.

Once the seeker himself has seen the Truth, he cannot help but sing its glory; he cannot help but sing what is life's opposite, and he cannot help but try to attract people to it. All this in accordance with the laws and rules in existence, whichever level of existence it may be. A spiritual master cannot invite anyone he desires to the feast, nor can he give knowledge to people who are not ready for it or destined to see that light. However, a spiritual master will continue to sing the pure song of good news, good news and only good news.

Every real Sufi master who has followed in the footsteps of the Prophet Muhammad has been tried and tested by Allah, just as all the prophets were tested, afflicted and denounced by many of their people. A Sufi master once said that a seeker will not reach the final step of real enlightenment unless some four hundred people who are considered to be good Muslims have renounced him. Many Sufis have been renounced by their wives, children and relations, but they never lost sight of the prime purpose of life which is arriving at knowledge of the Creator, and then passing on that knowledge to creation. In the Qur'an Allah says,

> Do men think that they will be left alone on saying, 'We believe', and not be tried? And certainly We tried those before them so that Allah will certainly know who are the sincere and who are the liars. (Qur'an 29.2–3).

Even when a person verbally acknowledges his belief in reality, Allah's mercy will come upon him to test him. He will also be tried because of his love of knowledge itself, which is one of the last and most difficult veils or barriers to be removed before true awakening takes place.

There are many Sufi anecdotes and sayings in this context. Shaykh Ahmad ibn Ata'illah al-Iskandari tells of how two people, a pious man and a sinner, went to the mosque to pray. When they came out of the mosque, the pious man was on his way to the eternal Fire of Hell, and the sinner to the everlasting Garden of Paradise. Commenting on this anecdote, Shaykh ibn Zarrukh says,

> The learned one was wrapped up in his own self-congratulatory state, for he was an upright person according to his own image

of himself, whereas the other man acknowledged that he was sinful and lowly and was ashamed of his ways. When they went to the mosque, each in his state, Allah's mercy descended upon the one who was wretched and needy of mercy. The sinner's repentance was accepted and Allah's mercy elevated him, whereas the so-called pious one was weighed down by his own self-praise and pride, so that Allah lowered him further to where he truly and deservedly belonged. Allah's attention was for the one whose cry for help was real. So when the two came out of the mosque, the one who was lowly and ashamed of his state and repentant became dear in the sight of his Lord, and he who made himself dear in his own eyes was cast out from his Lord's favours.

DREAMS AND VISIONS

Numerous Sufi masters have given attention to dreams and visions. The dream state has been recognised as an important dimension of life's experience. Dreams are of different types, and often reflect an aspect of the self. In most cases they relate to the material and mental level of the person. For a disciplined seeker, dreams can reflect higher and subtler meanings. The more spiritually refined one is, the more subtle will be the nature and the meaning of the dream. The more spiritually elevated a person is, the greater is the possibility of his receiving true dreams or visions. Sometimes dreams complement and interchange with the dreamer's physical reality. Once I dreamt of being injured in a car crash. Shaykh Bashir Uthman, who was a master of dream interpretation, told me that it is very testing to experience a crash, but this event had been transferred to the world of dreams instead of occuring in the physical world, so that I could experience the test without having to undergo actual physical injury.

MIRACLES

A miracle is generally an experience that is uncommon and unexplainable in the ordinary sense. If a seeker is exceptionally alert and sensitive spiritually, he can sometimes see the inter-relationship between the worlds of the seen and the unseen. When, later on, he reflects upon events which span both worlds and talks about them, his audience regards these events as miracles. People who are steeped in the inner realities continually connect between the seen and the unseen, for they do not separate the two, except in an intellectual sense for the purpose of verbal description. They are the people of unity. The greater a person's inner knowledge and awareness is, the less surprised he is about any outer events. In other words, the greater our vista of understanding is, the easier we can see the relationship between cause and effect in all occurrences, both in the seen and in the unseen.

In the history of the rise of man's consciousness, we find that the earlier messengers or prophets performed more miracles than the later ones. The one who especially performed many miraculous acts was the Prophet Jesus. One way to attract people's attention or to prove prophethood was to perform supernatural feats. All these events, however, belong to another more subtle natural order which can easily be understood by one who has insight into that dimension. Human consciousness has evolved during the last few thousand years, and has reached a point of alertness and intelligence where it no longer needs the shock treatment of miracles and unexplainable events in order to be convinced about the world of the unseen. The Prophet Muhammad did not profess to perform miracles except that of the Qur'an which was revealed to him in perfect Arabic through the Angel Gabriel despite his being unable to read or write. That is to say, he was not a conscious performer of miracles. His life and presence reflected the eternal truth which in itself is the greatest miracle.

Sufis throughout the ages have been concerned with unifying and understanding events, both in the seen and in the unseen. A few Sufi Orders have deviated from the original path of Islam and have become concerned with strange or mystical phenomena, often verging on mass hypnosis and mind control. Indonesia and some remote parts of Africa and the Far East have produced mystics who perform feats or illusions which are considered by onlookers to be miracles. As mentioned earlier, some spiritual masters from the Rifa'i Order are known to pierce their faces and other parts of their bodies with their swords without causing blood to be shed. One wonders how such unusual or mystical powers are attained, if at all! Are such abilities a help or a hindrance to the seeker?

One day an Indian sage with a most unusual talent was brought before Imam Jafar as-Sadiq. The spiritual leader was told that the man could see objects which were hidden behind any physical barrier. The spiritual leader put his hand in his pocket and asked the sage to inform him what he held in his hand. The Indian sage answered correctly. Imam Jafar as-Sadiq asked the sage how he had obtained this power. The sage replied that his strange vision had been cultivated as a result of his ego-lessness and by his always going against the wishes of his lower self. The spiritual leader acknowledged that the sage had achieved a great station and invited him to embrace Islam. The sage replied that he had an intense dislike for Islam. Iman Jafar as-Sadiq responded by pointing out that the sage had just said that he always opposed his ego and that if he hated a thing he would overcome his lower self by doing it. Should he therefore not accept Islam? The sage agreed and accepted the path of Islam, and the spiritual leader gave him the appropriate instructions and teaching. After a few weeks, the sage returned, very disturbed, and told the spiritual leader that throughout all his life he had constantly progressed to increasingly higher stations and had acquired greater and greater spiritual powers. However, since he had embraced Islam, he had now been completely stripped of his abilities and could not 'see' through physical barriers any more. He had been robbed of his powers by embracing Islam. What, he asked, was the explanation behind this? Imam Jafar as-Sadiq informed him that the laws of Reality are such, that for every virtue there is a reward. Everything in this existence is in perfect balance. Nothing goes unheeded. His worldly reward for his ego-lessness and his going against his lower self had been the gift of his 'X-ray' vision, but since he had entered the path of Islam, which encompasses both this world and the next, his reward for this high action, and all the high actions which resulted from it, would come in the next life. It is as though his span had been extended into another time zone, and so the Indian sage's station was now higher than it had been before, even though outwardly this did not seem to be the case.

So a great many powers or talents such as the one possessed by the sage can be acquired if a person seeks them and is willing to follow certain prescriptions and techniques. Such prescriptions have many parallels in Sufi practices and states. Many people who follow the Sufi path of self-renunciation or self-denial fall away from the true path when they begin to acquire such powers and consciously exhibit them. They then begin to dabble in practices concerned with the occult and unseen entities and spirits, and even in magic, which are diversions and distractions from the real aim of the true path, which is to arrive at gnosis of Allah. The sincere seeker who is guided by a genuine spiritual master avoids such diversions and distractions and does not stop until he reaches the true goal, and then goes on!

9 · SUFISM AND ORTHODOX ISLAM

Since the early history of Sufism, many conventional esoteric scholars of the religion of Islam and rulers have not tolerated the Sufis or their teachings. Sufis have been persecuted, denounced, exiled, imprisoned and in some cases even hanged or killed: Mansur al-Hallaj was hanged in 922; Yahya Suhra-wardi was killed mysteriously in the fort of Allepo in Syria in 1191; the works of Shaykh Ibn Arabi (d. 1240) were banned during his lifetime; Shaykh Ahmad ibn Ata'illah, the Shadhili Sufi master, (d. 1309) was severely confronted by Ibn Taymiyyah (d. 1328) who was a staunch enemy of Sufis; the great gnostic Mulla Sadra (d. 1640) was made an outcast for his teachings and ideas by the esoteric religious scholars of Persia; Shaykh Moulay al-Arabi ad-Darqawi (d. 1823) was imprisoned; and in more recent times, the ruler of Turkey, Kamal Ataturk (d. 1938), tried his best to wipe out all the Sufi Orders and Sufi sanctuaries in Turkey. In this context I asked the late Shaykh Muzzafar (d. 1986), the Sufi master of the Halveti-Jerrahi Order of Turkey, as to what happened after the almost complete destruction of the Sufi Orders in Turkey by Kamal Ataturk. He paused, smiled and said, 'You look upon it as destruction. We look upon it as slightly excessive grooming.' Then he continued, 'It is like chopping a grapevine to the ground. If he had chopped a little, the branches would have grown only a few metres away, but because he cut the whole grapevine to the ground, it will now grow all over the place. It is only a matter of time. Allah says in the Qur'an, 'They desire to put out the light of Allah with their mouths, and Allah will not consent save to perfect His light, though the unbelievers are averse' (Qur'an 9.32).

The conventional criticism and accusation levied against Sufis from within the Islamic community is that they care only for inner development, and are interested only in the unseen world, and that they neglect the outer laws of the Islamic Law and renounce the physical world. The path of original Islam is multi-dimensional and encompasses every aspect of life, outer as well as inner, for all these manifestations are part of one reality. There is one fundamental unifying factor behind all the visible and invisible worlds. The distinction between outer and inner, or gross and subtle, is only for the purpose of intellectual or practical discrimination, like distinguishing different colours on one horizon. People differ in taste and preference, and therefore some give more attention to the ritualistic aspects of the way of Islam, and some to its meaning or philosophical aspects. For lasting results a balance is necessary. Every human being contains an inner and an outer reality, and both require care and nourishment. Excessive attention to only one aspect could weaken the other, and the result when this happens is a lack of balance or harmony in a person's being. The same principle applies to society and to natural ecology. If gentle folk allow tyrants to rule over them, then oppression and destruction will be the outcome, instead of the kindness and tolerance which they advocate and desire to be the prevailing mode of life.

In accordance with the respective levels of people's spiritual potential, intellect, sincerity and sensitivity, we find that they care, to a greater or lesser extent, for the outer laws of the way of Islam, ritual and orthodoxy. Generally speaking, when people have protected themselves by adhering to the outer laws, their attention and interest can then be drawn more towards inner awakening and purification.

After the death of the blessed Prophet Muhammad (d. 632), Islamic codes began to be structured, formalised and centralised. Later on, the so-called Muslim kings and rulers, whose human and spiritual qualities were generally low, were not true followers of the prophetic norm of behaviour and way of life. Once this happened, as we have already seen, we begin to see the seeds of Sufism being sown. The greater the emphasis placed by these rulers and their adopted scholars of religion – whose concern was mainly for the outer Islamic Law and orthodoxy – on outer conformity, the more we find the needs of the reverse – inner qualities – being emphasised and beginning to manifest. The rise of Sufism came with the need to pay more attention to the inner – inner nourishment and satisfaction and inner awakening – in order to balance the outer orthodox rituals and outer laws.

As a result of this discrimination being made between inner and outer, and the loss of spontaneity of understanding of the original unific way of Islam, we find clashes occurring between the orthodox religious scholars and the Sufis, simply because, although both groups claimed they were following the way of Islam, their existential experience of life and their understanding of it, and therefore their actions and general behaviour, were different. These clashes were and are often cyclical, which signifies the duality and polarity of the outer law and the inner reality. Since everything is in its opposite, emphasis on the outer law will inevitably result in emphasis on the inner reality, just as emphasis on the inner reality will inevitably result in emphasis on the outer law. Very few people are able to maintain an even balance between the two.

Generally, the bias is more towards orthodoxy and the outer Islamic Law because it is easier to discuss them and apply them and uphold them. There is no doubt that some Sufis, like anyone else, may transgress some aspect of the outer Islamic Law, knowingly or unknowingly, at some time or other. It is said that if people did not have wrong actions, then how could Allah show His compassion and extend His forgiveness to them? However, there is an orthodoxy within Sufism itself, for like any movement which has a mainstream, there are also extremist Sufis. Furthermore, the pseudo-sufis are sometimes thought, mistakenly or intentionally, to be exemplars of the Sufi movement. However, the majority of the Sufis, especially the main Sufi Orders, uphold and apply all aspects of original Islam. They accept all the teachings and tenets of Islam and act upon them in all aspects, both outer and inner, the letter of the law as well as its spirit. So the Sufi is outwardly conformist and restricted, and inwardly exposed to the wide horizons of unrestricted freedom and bliss. There is a recorded saying attributed to Muhammad in this context:

> The outer law is my action,
> The path of purification is my way
> And the inner reality is my state.

So the Sufi's outer action is normality, commonality and orthodoxy, and his inner is a world which reflects the truth as Allah makes it available to him. He is watchful of what comes across his way because he believes that Allah is his Guide, his Nourisher and the One Who has brought him near to Him. The Sufi believes that Allah will guide him as appropriate, necessary and useful for him, and that after experiencing death, he will return to a new life which does not have any limitations and encumbrances as the life on this earth has.

Some orthodox Muslims consider the Sufis to be fatalists, and accordingly they say that if the Sufi teachings are followed, then society cannot progress. There has been much misunderstanding about the nature of the *Decree* and of *Destiny*, and the difference between them, since the earliest days of Islam. According to the Qur'an and the teaching of the Prophet Muhammad, it is on the Decree that natural laws are based, part of which we know, and part of which we have yet to discover. By means of these laws, balance and control is maintained over all the creational realities.

Allah has decreed that the whole creation is subject to the measure and extent of the laws that govern it. It is Allah's Decree, for example, that there is gravity and that every physical object or mass is subject to it. However, it is my destiny if I foolishly walk over the edge of the verandah and fall. So Destiny is the personalised experiential part of the Decree, that is, of the measures that control this existence. The Sufi understands the nature of the Decree and of Destiny, and the cause and effect chain operating throughout all the creational realities, of which his limited existence is an infinitesimal part. The purpose of existence is to align oneself along the destiny which has been prescribed, in the sense of following one's natural tendencies and behaving in accordance with one's natural environment with which we interact. This is not to say that one's destiny has been prescribed in an abstract or absolute sense, or in a controlled non-dynamic fashion, but in an interactive, multi-dimensional sense.

The way one normally acts in the world is by making an assessment of the outer situation and relating it to one's desire or objective and deducing an appropriate result. If the result is not as was desired, it means that there was an element missing in one's assessment. The Sufi is aware that the ultimate purpose of life is for him to constantly recognise the unity in creation whilst continually discriminating between this and that in all diverse experiences. True witnessing of this perfection can only occur when the individual reaches a state of submission and surrender willingly and knowingly. When this state is perfected, the individual personality melts with the total flow of events. For the person of total abandonment who transcends the cage of time and space, present and future become one. When Imam Husayn ibn Ali was leaving Mecca in 680 in order to travel to Kufa, rational advice was given to him that he would confront a great evil force if he attempted to make that journey, and that it would be better not to attempt it. Imam Husayn's reply to this counsel was, 'God has wished to see me martyred.' The spiritual leader had been given the privilege of seeing his destiny, for his spirit and consciousness were at such a level that he could witness what would happen to his body with complete detachment, contentment and submission. This is the way in which a truly enlightened person lives. It does not mean he is a fatalist. Rather, it means that he submits to the natural laws and

81

aligns himself with them in a manner that is appropriate to his natural make up and tendency and inherent characteristics. Iman Husayn fought to the end, and against all odds, whilst knowing clearly what the final outcome would be. Outer life is continuous struggle while inner light is uninterrupted bliss.

10 · THE ROLE OF THE SUFI

As we study the history of the spread of Islam throughout the last fourteen centuries, we find that, generally speaking, most of the Muslim rulers did not regard favourably the ways and practices of the Sufis. One obvious reason for this is that it is because the Sufis tried to check the un-Islamic way of life led by many Muslim rulers. Also, where the Sufis were successful in calling people to Islam, as was the case in Muslim Spain, it meant that there was a reduction in revenue to the government, since the new Muslims were no longer subject to certain taxes. Furthermore, with the usual zeal of the newly converted, they possessed greater clarity in recognising and not tolerating the un-Islamic behaviour of the rulers.

The way of Islam has spread partly through armed conquests, the purpose of which was often worldly gain and booty. From an early stage, the growing number of Muslims who were willing to fight for religion and wealth had to be satisfied. Many battles were fought for material wealth and the spoils of war. Others were fought in order to expand the dominion of the Muslims. Some Muslims fought in the way of Allah, convinced that what had been revealed to the Prophet Muhammad was a true guidance from God, and that anyone who rejected it should be fought, until they either accepted Islam or submitted to being governed by the Muslims.

However, Islam also spread as a result of the exemplary life led by Muslims, especially traders, who travelled and lived among non-Muslim populations. In the Far East, for example, Islam spread primarily through the Muslims and Arabs who traded there. In one incident, an Arab horse breeder in China raised and sold superior horses at a price lower than that demanded by the local breeders. When the Emperor investigated the complaints coming from the local horse-breeders, the Muslim defended himself by showing the Chinese ruler that his actions were of benefit to the entire community. Was he not adding to the wealth of the society by allowing more people to buy a better breed of animal at a price which they could afford? Furthermore, due to his skill and knowledge and his simple lifestyle, he was able to sell them at a lower profit and was quite content with his share. It is said that the ruler recognised the nobility and wisdom of the man's actions and accepted the Islamic way of life.

Another incident concerns a group of Sufis from North Africa who, while en route to China, stopped off in Southern Ceylon (now Sri Lanka) to repair their ships. The Buddhist king found their honesty, reliability and the quality of their courtesy and transactions of such a high standard that he encouraged them to stay on in Ceylon. Through this group of Sufis, the way of Islam began to spread throughout the country. Until this day, most of the Muslim population of Sri Lanka are called Moors. The original group of Sufis were members of the Shadhili Order and originated from Morocco. The first city which they built in Ceylon, located in the south-west of the island, was originally called Galee, which in Arabic means a castle. Today, the city is known as Galle. So Islam spread through people whose quality of life was higher than that of others.

Whenever there has been an opportunity to revolt against corrupt governments, the real Sufis have done so, and not always under the banner of Sufism. During the last three hundred years, the members of the Naqshbandi Order have played a most active political role. There are today active Naqshbandi movements in Russia. One heroic uprising was led by Imam Shamil from the Russian province of Khazakstan not very long ago. The Naqshbandi Sufis also played a significant role during the Independence movement in India prior to 1947. The circles of the Naqshbandi Sufis were strong, and they fought as Muslim soldiers in protest against British rule in India.

The Sufis lead a unified way of life and therefore they are concerned with the inner as well as the outer control of rulership. Thus it is ignorance on the part of those who say that the Sufi movement is an esoteric movement, and thereby attempt to relegate Sufism as being solely a way of life of retreat and monastic existence. This is not to say that there are not Sufis who primarily lead solitary existences due to particular circumstances or personal inclination. In normal circumstances, however, a Sufi is constantly driven to share the knowledge and light with which he has been gifted with others who deserve it. So a real Sufi is a person who has not wasted a single moment in following the divine prescription which is described in the Qur'an:

> We have sent you as a witness and as a bearer of good news and as a warner and as one inviting to Allah by His permission and as a light-giving torch. (Qur'an 33.45–46).

The difference between a prophet or a messenger and a Sufi or spiritual master is that a prophet or messenger receives divine communication directly from Allah, whereas a spiritual master receives it through the prophetic light. A prophet or messenger may also receive divine inspiration through other means, such as dreams or visions. The Prophet and Messenger of God, Muhammad, received communications through a direct means from Allah, which was the Archangel Gabriel. There is yet another mode of divine communication, which is called inspiration, which can be experienced by a receptive person.

The true Sufis have always followed the guidance of the Qur'an and the way of the Prophet Muhammad and have always understood that their vocation in this world is to witness the divine reality, to give the good news, and to guide people in the name of Allah to light upon light. They have always known the true path of Islam.

Sufism is the heart of Islam and is always at its best when it is not confined within any ethnic situation, when it is not Arabic Sufism, or Indian or Berber or Andalusian or Persian Sufism. We find that some of the greatest Sufi masters have not been confined to any ethnic group. They migrated in the way of Allah for learning and unfoldment somewhere completely different to their original culture. For example, Shaykh Abu'l-Abbas al-Mursi, who was originally from Murcia in Spain, pursued his spiritual quest in North Africa and eventually settled in Alexandria. Shaykh Muhiy'ud-Din Ibn Arabi, who was also from Murcia, travelled the Muslim lands of North Africa and the Arabian peninsula before ending his days in Damascus. Shaykh Mu'in'ud-Din Chisti travelled from Baghdad to Arabia, but settled in the Indian sub-Continent where he is now buried, in Ajmer and Shaykh Abdal-Qadir al-Gilani who eventually settled in Baghdad was originally from the city of Gilan in North Persia.

It is the original Islamic way of life which the true Sufis have always followed, transcending any ethnic, tribal or linguistic bias. They have followed the primal pattern of innate nature, which is the prophetic way, and which is to lead a life in accordance with the outer Islamic Law and to guide people to achieve the inner spiritual goal of self-fulfilment and contentment through self-enlightenment. Just as the way of Islam became a social reality and blossomed round the Prophet Muhammad, so it has always been given fresh life by the true Sufis, both in the places where Islam has been long established, and in the places where Islam is only just now arriving, for the price which they have to pay to receive the enlightenment which they desire is to teach people the primal way of original Islam.

11 · SUFISM AND SOCIETY

We define Sufism as the art or the way that leads man to being in full harmony and balance. It is the way which enables him to attain inner perception, understanding and therefore contentment in every situation in which he happens to be. The Sufi's interaction in all circumstances is in such harmony and in such unity with the total ecology that his actions appear as the manifestation of love and contentment in all circumstances. What appears to us to be an illness, to such a person is only a condition which is necessary in order to redress an imbalance. So he sees in it nothing other than deserved goodness and mercy. In a situation where he seems to us to be in constriction, he himself is in contentment and witnessing that state without objection. Inwardly he is always in a state of acceptance with knowledge and joy.

The inward state of a Sufi is what every human being wishes to attain, for the Sufi's position is at the pinnacle of the pyramid of society. If the Sufi is an integrated member of the community or of the society, and his nobility and virtues are recognised, then we find that he is respected and sought after as a guide or a teacher. His rank is considered above that of ordinary religious teachers or scholars.

In the early days of Islam, when spiritual qualities and values were dominant, the community's focal point was the mosque, and the teaching of Islam generated from it. Often we find that there were great teaching mosques in the bazaar area of the city, headed by the most knowledgeable men in the way of Islam and in Islamic Law. The great spiritual leaders of the communal prayer and the judiciary were connected closely with the mosque, because the life of the Muslims centred round their local mosques which were usually only a short distance from their houses. The grand mosque always had a teaching function as well as its other functions, such as the five daily obligatory prayers, the special Friday prayer and the twice-yearly festival prayers. All the main Islamic sciences were taught in the grand mosque, usually in a relatively structured manner, since a great deal of memorisation and learning by heart was involved. The teaching of the Sufis, on the other hand, was not based on an orthodox pattern, nor was it structured or centralised. Nevertheless, in a balanced situation these two forms of teaching complemented each other. There is nothing incompatible about learning a portion of Qur'an by heart and purifying the heart. Very often we find the spiritual leader of the central mosque taking guidance from a Sufi spiritual master who helps him in his inner struggle against his own ego in order to purify his lower self. Imam Khomeni writes that the greatest knowledge, inner experiences and self-knowledge were given to him by a Sufi spiritual master called Shah Abadi, to whom he refers repeatedly in several of his books. Shah Abadi was not known as a great scholar, or a renowned man of religious knowledge, or for possessing religious power, authority or fame. He was known to a small group of the religious elite and seekers of wisdom as a spiritual master of inner knowledge. Thus Sufis often exert considerable influence in society without being particularly noticed.

The extent of the Sufis' interaction with society has always depended very much upon their own personalities and on the economic, social, political and religious environment in which they happen to be living. We find that Sufi social behaviour varies considerably and widely, from their being unknown, quiet and seemingly ineffective persons, to their being in more or less visible positions of authority and leadership. Some Sufis have lived in the middle of a religious school, leading formal classes and producing other Sufi masters simultaneously. Others have lived in the outlying countryside, almost inaccessible to townspeople. A few have lived quietly in seclusion in remote mountain regions. Other Sufi masters alternate between spending time in the cities and in the countryside on a regular basis. Some Sufis have had only a few close followers, while others have had thousands. For example, Shaykh Sidi Ali al-Jamal's only really close follower appears to have been Shaykh Moulay al-Arabi ad-Darqawi, and yet from Shaykh ad-Darqawi literally hundreds of great men of wisdom and awakening, and many spiritual masters, emerged.

Occasionally we find some Sufi masters performing all the orthodox functions of the religious scholars, such as, for example, Shaykh Ahmad az-Zarruq who is buried in Libya. As well as being a great spiritual master, he was very learned in the outer Islamic Law. He defined the Sufi as a jurist who acts by his knowledge, and was highly critical of those people who claim to be Sufis but who do not follow the way of Islam.

Numerous Sufi masters have combined the functions of being the spiritual leader of a community as well as being a spiritual master with a circle of close followers, such as, for example Shaykh Uthman dan Fodio of Nigeria. We also find these Sufi spiritual leaders performing marriages and divorces and acting as judges, while, on the other hand, we also find many religious scholars and judges and other men concerned primarily with the outer Islamic Law, who have strong inclinations towards Sufism.

One requirement of life is to recognise all the aspects of creation within us, and to be in spontaneous awareness of the unitive nature of reality at all times. That is why one is constantly interested in the code of conduct prescribed by the Sufis. Throughout history, we find that every now and then, whenever the outer aspect, the physical and material, has been developed and stabilised, then man's attention has been drawn more towards the inner aspect of life. This is what gives rise to the periodic emergence of the Sufis and their influence in society. Also, when the outer circumstances of a society become intolerable, and its people are in confusion and suffering privation, and are in dire need of understanding the purpose of life, then again, we find man's attention turning towards knowledge and the search for a way out of such an intolerable situation.

It is in these situations that the Sufi centres and Sufi masters emerge. When excessive materialism, consumerism and decadence reach their zenith, then the situation demands the need to balance itself by turning towards establishing spiritual awareness and awakening, which is when Sufism begins to rise. Thus it is often the particular quality of life and its specific demands which determine the appropriate counter-balance needed to restore equilibrium.

The Sufis have often been misunderstood and sometimes persecuted. Therefore occasionally they have had to go underground in order to safeguard and continue their teaching discreetly. This has often been the result of the fear of tyrannical rulers or kings, or indeed even of the religious orthodoxy and power-mongering religious scholars who have felt that their religious authority and position in society were being challenged or undermined by the popularity of the Sufis. The Sufi way of freedom by submission to Allah's glorious unitive reality has often been a great challenge to those people who are worldly, and who have based their power on their ability to manipulate and assume authority in this world. This is because they are opposite each other in creation. The latter seek, love and worship power, and the former seek, love and worship the Source of power.

12 · SUFISM IN MODERN TIMES

During the eighteenth, nineteenth and early twentieth centuries, the major Sufi movements in Africa and Asia were often connected to mainstream Islamic movements. The Sufis were the elite of their societies, and often led the reform movements or opposition to oppression and foreign or colonial domination. Thus, for example, they were deeply involved in political movements such as the uprisings in Morocco and Algeria against the French, and the rebuilding of society and Islamic governance in Libya, which was carried out largely by members of the Sanusi Order. In northern Nigeria, Shaykh Uthman dan Fodio (d. 1817), a member of the Qadiri Order, led the religious war against the Habe rulers who had failed to govern according to the Islamic Law, which had led to the imposition of arbitrary taxes, general corruption, oppression and the dwindling of Islamic morality both at the popular and at the courtly levels. Further eastwards, Shaykh Muhammad Ahmad al-Mahdi (d. 1885), a member of the Tsemani Order, successfully opposed attempts at British colonial rule in Sudan. Similar phenomena occurred in the East as well. For example, the Naqshbandi Sufis and Shah Wali'ullah challenged the British colonial power in India.

Thus the Sufis were in action in many countries during the colonial era, opposing the colonial dismantling of Islamic governance and attempting to revive and sustain original Islam. They often formed or were at the heart of strong social groupings, and had great followings in many parts of the world. What kept many of these movements coherent and strong was the fact that during the nineteenth century people were not mobile, and the control or ownership of land, together with the influence of long-established cultural traditions, played an important role in the stability of society. However during the twentieth century, the situation began to change radically and rapidly.

The Western colonisation of most of the Muslim lands was almost complete by the end of the First World War. After that, the advent of secular and often Western appointed or approved 'client' rulers set the scene. Religious and Sufi interests and influences became of secondary importance, due to the rapid erosion of past and traditional values and lifestyles, and it became increasingly difficult and dangerous to follow the original way of Islam in its entirety in the Muslim lands. In contrast to what was happening in the East, we find many spiritual organisations and societies springing up in the West, often started by Western seekers of knowledge. The fact that many people from the Western societies embraced pseudo-religious movements, such as those of the Baha'i and Subud, as well as various branches of Buddhism, Hinduism and other minor new religions or revived versions of old ones, shows the growing thirst and interest in spiritual knowledge in the West, where the various versions of Christianity which were mind-or emotion-based, rather than 'heart'-based, had failed to provide any real spiritual nourishment for several centuries. More influential than these various movements were the Theosophist and Masonic movements. By the early twentieth century, we find that there was a great deal of interest in spiritualism in both Europe and North America.

The work of the orientalists who attempted to explore the spiritual dimension of the Eastern religions – albeit from within their own peculiar conceptual framework – including Islam, contributed to the increasing interest in spiritualism and the search for mystical experience in the West, by means of their writings and translations of original works on Eastern traditions, art, culture, philosophies and religions. Sufism began to arrive in the West alongside many other real or pseudo-spiritual movements. The arrival of so many Indian gurus and Buddhist masters coincided with the advent of interest in Sufism. By the middle of the twentieth century, we find quite a number of Sufi societies and movements springing up in Europe and North America, some of them founded by genuine Sufis and some by pseudo-sufis. As time went by, more information about Sufism and Islam on the whole became available in the West. The oil crisis in the West and the petrol boom in a number of Middle Eastern countries also helped in increasing contact with the Middle East and the Arabic language and information about Islam. Then came the revolution of the Islamic Republic of Iran in 1979 which has, ever since then, generated a global awakening of interest in the Islamic tradition. It will not be out of context to mention here that Imam Khomeni's former residence and the place where he gave audience to his people in the north of Tehran is itself a Sufi mosque and sanctuary. In fact Imam Khomeni concentrated on the science of Sufism and gnosis during his early years at the religious school in Qum, and his early writings were mainly concerned with the inner meaning of night vigils, night prayers and self-awakening.

It is important that we do not confuse the spiritual qualities of an individual with outer events. Imam Ali, the master of all Sufis, had only war on his hands during his years as the leader of the Muslim community. Outer events can sometimes confuse the onlooker and conceal the light of such beings.

As for the state of Sufism in the West in the more recent past, we observe in conclusion that many of the groups that had accepted Sufism in order to benefit from some of its disciplines, doctrines, practices or experiences have begun to disintegrate. These groups of the 'new age' movement which embraced a number of ideas derived from Sufism are breaking apart because their way of life is not in harmony with the mainstream of original Islam, and accordingly they do not have the outer protection which is necessary to protect and ensure the safety of the inner movement. Thus during the last few decades of this century, we observe that most Sufi movements in the West have either been strengthened by holding on to the outer practices of Islam, or weakened and degenerated by not doing so.

13 · SUFI BIOGRAPHIES

We have selected these Sufis, not on account of their greatness, for that is only known to Allah, but simply because they represent diverse cultural, educational and vocational backgrounds and also because the author is familiar with them. They are not arranged in any special order.

RABI'A AL-ADAWIYA

Rabi'a al-Adawiya (d. 801) is one of the most famous Sufis of Basra, in present-day Iraq. She was born into a very poor family. When both her parents died, she was sold into slavery, but was later set free by her master due to her asceticism and piety.

Rabi'a's love and passion for Allah was so intense that there was no room left in her heart or mind for any other thought or interest. She did not marry, and the world meant nothing to her. She shut her window in spring without looking out onto the flowers, and became lost in contemplation of the all-encompassing Creator of all. Addressing God in poetical abandon she says:

O Beloved of hearts, I have none like You,
So have pity this day on the sinner who comes to You.

O my Hope and my Rest and my Delight,
The heart can love none other than You.

For Rabi'a the only thing that mattered was absorption in
Allah, putting all her hope in God and losing herself in His
praise. The nightly prayer became for her a sweet and loving
conversation between her and her Beloved.

Once Rabi'a asked Sufyan ath-Thawri, a Sufi of Basra,
'What is your definition of generosity?' He replied, 'For this
world's inhabitants, generosity consists in giving away one's
possessions; for those of the world beyond, generosity amounts
to sacrificing one's self.' Rabi'a disagreed strongly, saying that
he was mistaken. According to her, generosity is to worship
God out of love for Him alone, and not in order to receive any
reward or benefit in return.

In the history of Sufism, Rabi'a has become a legend,
epitomising devotional adoration along the path of asceticism
and love.

SAYYIDA NAFISAH

Sayyida Nafisah was the great grand-daughter of Imam Hasan,
the son of Imam Ali, and was among the first of the family
of the Prophet Muhammad to leave the Arabian Peninsula
and resettle in what is now the outskirts of modern Cairo in
Egypt. She was a woman who was renowned for her piety,
asceticism, night vigils and prayers, and widely reputed for
her saintliness and mystical powers. Imam Shafi'i, the Sunni
jurist and founder of one of the four famous schools of Sunni
Islamic Law, was only one of the many religious scholars of
his day to discuss spiritual matters with her. When he died in
820, his body was taken to her house so that she might recite
prayers for him over it.

When Sayyida Nafisah died in 824, her husband, the son of
Imam Ja'far as-Sadiq, wanted to take her body back to Medina
to bury her there. However the people of her village, which was
called Fustat, begged her husband to let her be buried there
so that they would continue to benefit from her blessing and
grace. She was laid to rest in her house in a grave which she

had dug with her own hands many years earlier. It is reported that among her many devotional acts which she performed during her lifetime, was the reading of six thousand complete recitations of the Qur'an while sitting in that grave. The spot on which her house stood is now occupied by her mausoleum and mosque. This tomb has a great reputation, since experience has shown that supplications which are made to Allah near it are answered. Streams of visitors make their way to her shrine every day, and especially on Fridays, filling the mosque and the surrounding courtyards.

IMAM JUNAYD AL-BAGHDADI

Imam Junayd al-Baghdadi (d. 910) was born in Nihawand in Persia, but his family settled in Baghdad where he studied Islamic Law according to the school of Imam Shafi'i, and eventually became the chief judge in Baghdad. In Sufi discipline, he was the close follower of his uncle, Shaykh as-Sari as-Saqti. Although he was the spiritual master of Mansur al-Hallaj, he was obliged, in his capacity as chief judge of Baghdad, to sign the warrant authorising the execution of al-Hallaj. On it he wrote, 'Under Islamic Law, he is guilty. According to the Inner Reality, Allah knows.'

Due to the antagonism of orthodox religious scholars against the Sufis, Imam Junayd performed his spiritual practices and taught his close followers behind seven locked doors. From his letters, short treatises and the accounts of later Sufis and Sufi biographers, we gather that for him the Sufi way of life meant the permanent striving to return to one's Source, which is God, and from which everything proceeds. For him, spiritual love meant that, 'The qualities of the Beloved replace the qualities of the lover.'

Imam Junayd concentrated all thought and inclination, every admiration, every hope and every fear, on God. He is considered to be the undisputed master of the Sufis of Baghdad. Many Sufi Orders trace their chain of transmission of knowledge from master to master back through him. It is related that he said:

> We did not take *Sufism* from talk or words, but from hunger and detachment from the world, and by leaving the things to which we were habituated and which were agreeable to us.

and

> If I had known of any science greater than *Sufism*, I would have gone to it, even on my hands and knees.

and

> God purifies the 'heart' of a person according to the measure of the sincerity of a person in remembering Him.

Imam Junayd was once asked, 'Who is a gnostic?' He replied, 'The one who is not bound by time.'

MANSUR AL-HALLAJ

Mansur al-Hallaj was born in the province of Fars in Persia in 858. His father was a cotton carder, which is the meaning of the word *hallaj*. He was the close follower of several well-known Sufis of his time, including Sahl at-Tustari of Basra, Amr al-Makki and Imam Junayd of Baghdad. However, later on, on account of his saying *'Ana'l Haqq'*, meaning 'I am the Truth', he was accused of propagating an unacceptable and dangerous religious claim, for which he was executed by the orthodox establishment in 922. From the surviving fragments of his work, we surmise that he was a Sufi intoxicated with divine love. His poetry is a very tender and intense expression of spiritual yearning and love. For example, he sang:

> Kill me, O my trustworthy friends,
> For in my being killed is my life.

Love is, in fact, the central theme of Mansur al-Hallaj's prayers and sayings. Describing divine love, he says:

> Love is that you remain standing in front of your Beloved:
> When you are deprived of all your attributes,
> Then His attributes become your qualities.

The later Sufis, until our own time, have quoted Mansur al-Hallaj as being the epitome of those intoxicated by divine love.

IMAM ABU HAMID AL-GHAZZALI

Imam Abu Hamid al-Ghazzali was born in Tus in north-east Persia in 1058, three years after the Seljuks had taken over the rulership in Baghdad. He followed the traditional course of theological studies based on the study of the Qur'an, the recorded actions and sayings of the Prophet Muhammad, and Islamic Law according to the school of Imam Shafi'i. In the course of time, he was appointed as a professor at the Nizamiyya religious school in Baghdad, where he taught theology and Islamic Law.

In 1095, Imam al-Ghazzali went through a severe inner breakdown, a spiritual crisis, and so, having ensured that his family was well provided for, he left his teaching position to enter the spiritual life. He encountered many Sufis during his travels and underwent several spiritual disciplines. Later on, he returned to his home town, now a completely transformed man, and resumed his teaching up until his death in 1111.

Imam al-Ghazzali's book called *Revival of the Religious Sciences* is considered to be his greatest work. It is the fruit of his religious scholarship combined with his inner spiritual experience. His teaching and preaching after his inner awakening consisted of the transmission of the inner sciences and the integration of Sufi practices with strict adherence to the outer Islamic Law. This made him one of the most influential theologians in the Muslim world, as well as making the orthodox religious scholars take Sufi movements seriously.

One of his famous sayings is, 'Those which are learned about, for example, the laws of divorce, can tell you nothing about the simpler aspects of spiritual life, such as the meaning of sincerity towards God or trust in Him.'

SHAYKH MUHIY'UD-DIN IBN ARABI

Shaykh Muhiy'ud-Din Ibn Arabi was born in Murcia in southeast Spain in 1165. His father was a close follower of Shaykh Abdal-Qadir al-Gilani and a renowned and respected person. In his childhood he was taught religious sciences by two women saints, Yasmin of Marchena and Fatima of Cordova. When he was eight, his family moved to Seville where he studied the science of the Qur'an and the recorded actions and sayings of the Prophet Muhammad. By the time he was nineteen, he had already been in seclusion and spiritual retreat with considerable success. From then on, he began receiving visions and witnessing the descent of divine effulgence upon him. He stayed in Andalusia and North Africa until 1198, meeting many Sufis and various religious scholars.

In 1201 Shaykh Ibn Arabi travelled to Mecca for the pilgrimage. At that time he prayed to God and asked Him to reveal to him all that was to happen in the material and spiritual worlds. He has recorded what he experienced in these realms in his written works, especially *The Makkan Revelations* and *The Seals of Wisdom*. Even in his own time Shaykh Ibn Arabi was considered to be a great philosopher, a prolific gnostic writer and an accomplished Sufi spiritual teacher, and the books of his that survive still excite a great deal of interest today.

Undoubtedly Ibn Arabi held the orthodox religious scholars in contempt. He made no secret of his disgust at their ignorance and lack of inner effulgence and spiritual enlightenment, which gave rise to his denunciation and arrest in 1206. He was at that time in Cairo, living in the company of a small group of Sufis. He was forced to flee to Mecca and from there to Qonya, where he met a young Sufi called Sadr'ud-Din Qunawi whose mother he married. He eventually settled down in Damascus until his death in 1240.

It is said that one day, shortly before his death, Shaykh Ibn Arabi confronted some religious scholars and said, 'What you worship is under my feet.' His words enraged them, especially since they did not understand them. After his death and his funeral, these same men decided to dig up his body and move it. They had not been digging at one end of the grave for long, before they uncovered a cache of gold, concealed just below the dead master's feet!

Shaykh Ibn Arabi was a prolific writer. Various traditional sources have attributed several hundred works to him. It is not possible to describe the degree or extent of his influence upon Sufism, except to say that after him there was practically no exposition of Sufi doctrine which did not come in one way or another under the influence of his works. Shaykh Ibn Arabi is buried north of Damascus, and his shrine is a centre of pilgrimage and Sufi gatherings to this day. Among his sayings are:

Take your knowledge only from the one who acts by it.

and

Whoever engages in travel will arrive!

MAWLANA JALAL'UD-DIN RUMI

Mawlana Jalal'ud-Din Rumi was born in Balkh in present day Afghanistan in 1207. His father Baha'ud-Din, was a noted theologian and Sufi. In 1220, when Balkh was threatened by the invading hordes of Mongols from central Asia, Baha'ud-Din and his family left Balkh and, travelling via Khurasan and Syria, reached the province of Rum in central Anatolia, which is in present-day Turkey. They settled in Qonya, the capital of Rum, and soon Baha'ud-Din's teaching and preaching met with great success, even attracting Sultan Ala'ud-Din Kaykubad. Jalal'ud-Din was brought up in his father's tradition of learning, and after his father's death, he was introduced to direct knowledge of God and the deeper mysteries of spiritual life by Shaykh Burhan'ud-Din Muhaqiq al-Tirmidhi. Under Shaykh al-Tirmidhi's guidance, Rumi underwent many spiritual retreats of forty days each, until he was awakened and enlightened.

In 1244 Rumi met another spiritual master, Shams'ud-Din of Tabriz, who transformed him completely. There was measureless love between the two. After Shams'ud-Din's death, Rumi met several more spiritual masters. It was one of his close followers, Husam'ud-Din Chalabi who inspired Rumi to record his entire wisdom on paper for his followers. Rumi acceded to this wish and started dictating his famous *Mathnavi-ye Ma'navi* to Husam'ud-Din, which continued until his death in 1273. The *Mathnavi* is considered by the Sufis to be a spiritual commentary on the Qur'an in the Persian language. For example, Mawlana Jalal'ud-Din Rumi says:

> Every prophet has received from Him the guarantee:
> Seek help with patience and prayer.
> Come, ask of Him, not anyone except Him.
> Seek water in the sea; do not seek it in the dry river-bed.

and

> What is unification?
> To burn one's self before the One.

and

> I have remained for the sake of betterment
> In the prison of this world.
> What have I to do with the prison?
> Whose money have I stolen?

MULLA SADRA

The Safavid period in Persia was one of the most active periods in the intellectual and gnostic life of Islam. During this period, the most debated issue in the Muslim intellectual world was the relationship between science and faith. The harmonious blending and integration of science and faith, and reason and revelation, was the contribution of the prolific philosopher and gnostic, Sadr'ud-Din Shirazi, usually known as Mulla Sadra.

Mulla Sadra was born in Shiraz in Persia in 1571, into a wealthy and influential Shi'ite family, and received his early education in that city which was then one of the most important cultural centres of the country. After completing his early training, he set out for Ispahan, the capital and intellectual centre of Persia at that time, in order to complete his formal education. There he studied with the leading authorities of the day, learning the religious sciences from Baha'ud-Din Amili and the intellectual sciences from Mir Damad. Having completed his formal education, he retired from worldly life and withdrew to a small village called Kahak, near Qum, where he spent about seven years undergoing spiritual practices and the discipline of much remembrance of Allah for the purification of his soul, which led to his self-realisation and awakening. He finally emerged as an illuminated sage.

Having thus perfected both the outer and inner aspects of knowledge, Mulla Sadra returned to active life, becoming a professor at the Khan religious school of Shiraz where he taught transcendental philosophy for the rest of his life. He died in the city of Basra in 1640 while returning from the pilgrimage to Mecca.

Mulla Sadra's school of thought is known as transcendental wisdom and has produced many learned gnostics in Persia up until recent times. Since he wrote in a simple style and openly expounded gnostic and metaphysical doctrines, he was soon exposed to the attacks of the orthodox religious scholars, some of whom even accused him of having gone out of Islam, despite his following the outer Islamic Law as well as having access to and talking about the inner reality.

Mulla Sadra's basic thesis is that in order to gain perfect knowledge of things, one's rational knowledge should be combined with spiritual tasting, and one's theoretical knowledge should be combined with the realisation of higher consciousness, which is a gift by the grace of God, attained by those who purify their souls by following the Muhammadi way of life.

KHWAJA MU'IN'UD-DIN CHISTI

The Chisti Order, probably the most widespread and influential of the Sufi Orders in the sub-continent of India, was introduced into India by Khwaja Mu'in'ud-Din Chisti, popularly known as Hazrat Gharib Nawaz which means the Helper of the Poor. He was born in about 1142 in Seistan in central Asia, and was descended from both Imam Hasan and Imam Husayn. He studied the traditional Islamic sciences of the Qur'an and the recorded actions and sayings of the Prophet Muhammad in the universities of Bukhara and Samarkand. However, his yearning for the inner knowledge of self-unfoldment led him to become the close follower of Khwaja Uthman Herwani, a Chisti Sufi master from the Nishapur region of Khurasan in Persia. He served this spiritual master devotedly for twenty years, accompanying him on many travels throughout central Asia and Arabia. After going on the pilgrimage to Mecca, and visiting the tomb of Muhammad in Medina, he was asked to establish Islam in India. After spending forty days in spiritual retreat next to the tomb of Shaykh Hujwiri (d. about 1075) in Lahore, Shaykh Chisti made his way to India.

Hazrat Gharib Nawaz was nearing fifty when he reached India. After his stay in Lahore, he travelled via Multan and Delhi until he arrived in Ajmer in Rajasthan which he made his base. Here he is said to have married twice, although he had previously remained celibate. One of his wives came from a Muslim background, while the other was of Hindu origin, and both gave him children. In Ajmer he devoted most of his time to guiding serious seekers of self-knowledge, and to dispelling the ignorance of the orthodox Muslims by awakening a higher consciousness of the reality of Islam in them. He also inspired many Hindus to purify their own devotional practices, and there is no doubt that many people's hearts turned to Islam because of the example which he himself set. Some historical accounts state that forty thousand families accepted Islam at his hand.

Shaykh Mu'in'ud-Din Chisti died in 1236. His teaching was quite simple and basic, and he preached in a manner that was universal rather than purely dogmatic. He taught that the highest form of devotion was nothing other than 'feeding the hungry, providing clothes for the naked and helping those in distress'. He describes the qualities that endear man to God as being 'river-like generosity, sun-like affection and earth-like hospitality'.

The proof of the universality of Hazrat Gharib Nawaz's message and his role as a teacher is that today, as throughout all the centuries since his death, his tomb in Ajmer is visited by innumerable Muslims and countless thousands of Hindus who acknowledge his high spiritual station. Every day, all the year round, as in his lifetime, gifts of food from the more well-off flood into the hands of his descendants, only to be cooked in giant cauldrons and redistributed to the less well-off before the end of the day.

SHAYKH NIZAM'UD-DIN AWLIYA

Shaykh Nizam'ud-Din Awliya, who is considered the greatest Sufi master of medieval India, was born in Bada'un in North India in 1238 into a family whose genealogy traced back to the Prophet Muhammad and who had originated from Bukhara. He studied the sciences of Islamic Law in order to qualify as a judge, but in about 1257 was inspired to travel to Ajodhan to visit Shaykh Farid'ud-Din Ganji Shakar, the most celebrated Chisti spiritual master of that time. There his destiny changed. He became the close follower of this spiritual master, and on his third and final visit to Ajodhan Shaykh Farid'ud-Din designated him as his successor. He advised him to continue with his studies of the Qur'an and Islamic jurisprudence, alongside his supererogatory prayers and the pursuit of the sufic sciences, and to devote himself to whichever finally won the upper hand.

Shaykh Nizam'ud-Din eventually settled down in Ghiyaspur near Delhi. There he established his Sufi sanctuary which became a focal point for the spiritual renewal of the lives of the people of Delhi. Shaykh Nizam'ud-Din personally led a life of celibacy and asceticism. He and his close followers subsisted on unasked for charity which they distributed every day to the neighbouring poor, so that by the end of each day they had nothing stored up for the next day. His simple, basic teaching attracted people from all walks of life, including members of the sultan's family and his court. However, he refused to visit or meet the then ruler of the Delhi sultanate. 'There are two doors in my sanctuary,' said Shaykh Nizam'ud-Din, 'and if the Sultan enters through one of them, I will go out through the other.'

The fame of Shaykh Nizam'ud-Din became so widespread that wells were dug along the route between Delhi and Ghiyaspur, water vessels kept ready, carpets spread, awnings erected and a man who knew the entire Qur'an by heart stationed at every resting place, so that the people going to visit him should not suffer any inconvenience on their journey. Owing to the fame and wisdom of the spiritual master, many Muslims in the country inclined towards the Sufi way of life, and in time, there were so many Sufi sanctuaries in India that it was possible for a wandering Sufi to travel from sanctuary to sanctuary, spending three days at each sanctuary, without ever staying in the same sanctuary twice in the space of a year.

Shaykh Nizam'ud-Din's respect for the devout Hindus, for whom his doors were always open, is shown by his comment to his close follower, the famous poet Amir Khusraw, when watching some of them at their devotional practices: 'Every community has its own path and faith and its own way of worship.' It was through Amir Khusraw, that the practice of *quwali*, which is the singing of the praises of Allah and the Prophet Muhammad and his family and companions, accompanied by music, was developed and perfected.

Shaykh Nizam'ud-Din said, 'The way to me is through Amir Khusraw.' When Amir Khusraw returned from a journey to find that Shaykh Nizam'ud-Din had died while he was away, he immediately died from grief on the spot, and was buried only a few yards away from his spiritual master. Ever since then, the tombs of these two saints have always been covered in rose-petals, scattered by the innumerable visitors who flock to visit them. Under the leadership of 'the master of the spiritual masters', as Shaykh Nizam'ud-Din Awliya was commonly known, the Chisti Order had a great impact on the lives of the people of Delhi, and after his death in 1325, it spread throughout the rest of the Indian sub-continent.

SHAH WALI'ULLAH

Shah Wali'ullah, the great Muslim reformer of eighteenth-century India, was born in 1702 into a family that had already produced many Muslim scholars, especially his father, Shah Abdur-Rahim, who had founded the Rahimiyya centre for religious learning in Delhi. Shah Wali'ullah's father supervised his son's Islamic education, and before his death in 1719, he appointed Shah Wali'ullah as the head of his religious school and initiated him into the Naqshbandi Order.

During his visit to Mecca on the pilgrimage in 1730, Shah Wali'ullah claims to have received a vision of Muhammad in which his station as a divinely appointed reformer for his people was revealed to him. At this stage in the history of Islam, the lack of a vibrant, living Islam in India had contributed towards a situation in which the corrupt Mughal Empire was disintegrating amidst the growing power of the Hindus and the Sikhs and the increasing influence of the British East India Company. Shah Wali'ullah saw in the lives of Muhammad and his Family and Companions the key to a correct code of behaviour whereby a renaissance of Islam in his own country could be achieved. On his return to India in 1732, he directed his efforts towards re-establishing a simple Arab-style Islam, purified of the Turkish, Persian and Hindu cultural elements which had become prevalent amongst the Muslims in India at that time.

Shah Wali'ullah was a strong Sunni Muslim who was attracted to the teaching of Imam Malik in his *Al-Muwatta*. He displayed a critical anti-Shi'a stance, which may in part have arisen as a result of the distorted Shi'a practices which were prevalent in his time in the sub-Continent, and his lack of exposure to the original Shi'a teachings. He said that one of the books which would be the key to establishing Islam in the West would be *Ash-Shifa* of Qadi Iyad.

Shah Wali'ullah expanded the work of his father by making the Rahimiyya religious centre not only a training ground for men of knowledge, but also a 'think tank' where the spiritually motivated could, under his guidance, plan the revival of Islam in India. He found nothing incompatible in combining the roles of Sufi and scholar of Islamic Law in his own life, and worked assiduously to bridge the gap which existed between some sufis and religious scholars. He counselled the would-be Sufi to learn first to obey all the laws of Islam, and to avoid unnecessary dissipation of energy by selecting one school of Islamic Law and adhering to it. The sincere seeker should then progress to obeying his spiritual master. He should dedicate himself to a life of prayer, fasting, remembrance of God and the recitation of the Qur'an, while continuing to observe and honour his obligations to the surrounding Muslim community. He was equally concerned with the existential behaviour of the Muslims in general. He considered a state of economic equilibrium necessary for the spiritual health of the nation, and publicly protested against the prevalent imbalance of wealth and crippling taxation which characterised the tail-end of Mughal rule.

After his death in 1762, Shah Wali'ullah's work was continued both by the members of his family and by his close followers, the chief of whom was his son, Shah Abdal-Aziz, who took over the running of the Rahimiyya religious school. Although more than two centuries have passed since his death, Shah Wali'ullah's life is still the subject of much discussion and study.

SHAYKH ABU'L-HASAN ASH-SHADHILI

Shaykh Abu'l-Hasan ash-Shadhili was born in the north of Morocco in 1175 into a family of peasant labourers. For his education he went to the Qarawiyyin University in Fes, where he met some scholars who introduced him to the sciences of Islamic Law. He also travelled to many countries. In Iraq he met a great Sufi called Wasiti who told him to return to his country where he would find Moulay Abdas-Salam ibn Mashish, the great Moroccan spiritual master. He did so, and became the close follower of this spiritual master who initiated him in the way of remembrance of Allah and enlightenment. When he met Moulay Abdas-Salam after ritually washing himself, he said, 'O Allah, I have been washed of my knowledge and action so that I do not possess knowledge or action except what comes to me from this Shaykh.'

Shaykh Abu'l-Hasan ash-Shadhili travelled from Morocco to Spain and finally settled down in Alexandria. Later on in life, when asked who his spiritual master was, he used to reply, 'I used to be the close follower of Moulay Abdas-Salam ibn Mashish, but I am no more the close follower of any human master.' Shaykh Abu'l-Abbas al-Mursi (d. 1288), who succeeded Shaykh ash-Shadhili as the next spiritual master of the Order, was asked about the knowledge of his spiritual master and replied, 'He gave me forty sciences. He was an ocean without a shore.'

Shaykh ash-Shadhili had hundreds of close followers in both Alexandria and Cairo, not only from among the common people but also from among the ruling classes. He taught his close followers to lead a life of contemplation and re-membrance of Allah while performing the normal everyday activities of the world. He disliked initiating any would-be follower unless that person already had a profession. His admonition to his close followers was to apply the teachings of Islam in their own lives in the world and to transform their existence.

Shaykh Abu'l-Hasan Ash-Shadhili died in the south of Egypt near the Red Sea while he was on his way to the pilgrimage in Mecca in 1258. His shrine, which appears to be nowhere, in the middle of the desert, stands to the present day and is highly venerated. Near his tomb are two wells, one containing sweet water, the other containing bitter water. He was an interspace between two seas, the sea of the outer law and the sea of the inner reality. The Shadhili Order derives its name from him. He said:

> O Allah, You have sentenced the people to abasement until they become mighty, and You have sentenced them to loss until they find. The one who has no abasement becomes the one who has no might, and the one who has no loss becomes the one who has no finding. The one who lays claim to finding without abasement is deluded. The one who lays claim to finding without loss is a liar.

SHAYKH TAJ'UD-DIN AHMAD IBN ATA'ILLAH

Shaykh Taj'ud-Din Ahmad ibn Ata'illah was born in about 1250 into a distinguished family of religious scholars who followed the school of Imam Malik in Alexandria. His father was a close follower of Shaykh Abu'l Hasan ash-Shadhili. Ahmad ibn Ata'illah became the close follower of Shaykh Abu'l-Abbas al-Mursi after he had completed his study of Islamic Law as transmitted by the school of Imam Malik. Shaykh Abu'l-Abbas al-Mursi predicted that Ahmad ibn Ata'illah would become an authority in both the Sufi path and Islamic Law, and it was in Cairo that this prediction of his future greatness came true, for there he led two lives. One was his professional life as a teacher of Islamic Law in accordance with what had been transmitted through Imam Malik in various public institutions and mosques in Cairo, such as Al-Azhar and the newly built Al-Mansuriyyah, together with his public preaching which attracted large audiences; his other life was devoted to his duties as a spiritual master of the Shadhili Order, in which he transmitted the transformative teaching of the Muhammadi code to sincere seekers of wisdom and gnosis. Shaykh Ahmad ibn Ata'illah was also influential in the Mamluk court, and used to counsel Sultan al-Mansur (d. 1298) on religious matters.

Towards the end of his life, Shaykh Ahmad ibn Ata'illah was confronted by a well-known religious scholar called Ibn Taymiyyah (d. 1328) who was a stark enemy of all sufis. With reference to him, Shaykh Ahmad ibn Ata'illah warned everyone about the shallow-minded attitude displayed by some orthodox jurists and religious scholars towards Sufism. He died in 1309, and his tomb in the Qarafah cemetery in Cairo, where many people have experienced miraculous phenomena, still stands to this day. Some of Shaykh Ahmad ibn Ata'illah's wise sayings are:

> Do not travel from created being to created being.
> Otherwise you will be like the donkey at the mill-stone:
> That from which he travels is that to which he travels.
> Rather travel from created beings to the Maker of being:

'And the final end is to your Lord.'

Your turning to Allah is your turning away from creation.
Your turning to creation is your turning away from Allah.

Do not keep the company of anyone
Whose state does not inspire you,
And whose speech does not guide you to Allah.

The heart does not benefit by anything like withdrawal
By which it enters the arena of reflection.

And, quoting Shaykh Abdal-Qadir al-Gilani:

I did not reach Allah the Exalted by standing in prayer at night,
nor by fasting in the day nor by studying knowledge. I reached
Allah by generosity and humility and soundness of the heart.

He also said:

Allah has a garden in this world.
Whoever enters it does not yearn
For the garden of the Next World.

and

You are not veiled from Allah by the existence of something
that exists with Him since there is nothing which exists with
Him. You are veiled from Him by the illusion that something
exists with Him.

SHAYKH MOULAY AL-ARABI AD-DARQAWI

Shaykh Moulay al-Arabi ad-Darqawi was born around the
middle of the eighteenth century in a village near Fes in
Morocco. He studied the Qur'an and Islamic Law under
the guidance of the traditional teachers in his village, and
then went to Fes, where he met many religious scholars of
Islamic Law, as well as some of the spiritual masters of inner
unfoldment, but not yet his real master.

When he realised that he needed a spiritual master to guide
him, Moulay al-Arabi went to the shrine of Moulay Idris, a
great saint who is buried in Fes, and began to recite the

111

Qur'an with the intention of receiving divine help in finding his spiritual guide and master. When, after the sixth recitation of the Qur'an, there was still no indication and he became heartbroken and desolate, Allah's grace came upon him, and he met Moulay al-Imrani, who was known as Sidi Ali al-Jamal, in 1767. He said, 'O master, I have been looking for a Shaykh for a long time.' Sidi Ali al-Jamal replied, 'And I have been looking for a sincere follower for a very long time.' Among the sayings of Sidi Ali al-Jamal which Shaykh ad-Darqawi quotes in his letters are the following:

Would that You were sweet while this life is bitter.
Would that You were pleased while people are angry.
Would that what is between You and me
Were filled and flourishing, and that
What is between me and the world were a ruin.
If Your love proves true,
Then all is easy, and all which is on earth is earth.

Were it not for the fire and the bee-sting,
The pleasure of the honeycomb and the honey
Would not be perfect.

When people are occupied with worship,
Then you should be occupied with the Worshipped.
When they are occupied with love,
Be occupied with the Beloved.

After the death of Sidi al-Jamal in 1779, Moulay al-Arabi ad-Darqawi became the next spiritual master of the Order, with some 40,000 people as his followers. His followers were from all over North Africa, and his order came to be known as the Shadhili-Darqawi Order. His influence was so great that he was imprisoned by one of the rulers of his time, until that ruler died and the next ruler released him. He lived to be about eighty years old and died in a village called Bu Barih, which is in the mountains north of Fes, in 1823. His shrine is visited by very many people, and a great festival of remembrance of Allah is held there every year.

The teachings of Shaykh Moulay al-Arabi ad-Darqawi were simple and based on adherence to the way of Islam, appropriate ethical actions, noble character, modesty, silence, contemplation, doing without, poverty and abasement before Allah. For twenty-five years, he and his family lived from day to day, never storing up any food for the next day, but, like the birds who have nothing at the beginning and end of each day, trusting completely in Allah for all their needs to be met. A large part of his teaching deals with overcoming the lower self. Some of his sayings are:

> Sufism is observing the outer law of the way of Muhammad, surrendering the will to the Lord of the worlds, and having good character towards the Muslims.

> The Sufi is the one who is not saddened when he lacks something, great or small.

And, quoting Sidi Ali al-Jamal:

> Had people known what secrets and blessings
> There are in need,
> They would not need anything except need.

> Exposed yourselves to the fragrant breezes of Allah.

> Do not say, 'I am nothing.' Do not say, 'I am something.'
> Do not say, 'Something concerns me.' Do not say, 'Nothing concerns me.' Say, 'Allah', and you will see wonders.

> Beware of the company of three types of people:
> Heedless tyrants, hypocritical Qur'an recitors,
> and ignorant sufis.

And, quoting Imam Malik:

> Whoever has the outer Law without the inner Reality
> has left the right way;
> Whoever has the inner Reality without the outer Law
> is a heretic;
> Whoever joins the two of them has realisation.

He also said:

113

There is a knowledge beyond written transmission which is finer than the ultimate perception of sound intellects.

Books do not contain the cure of the hearts.
Hearts are cured by the company of the lords of the hearts.
The knowledge of books is a residue from the knowledge of
hearts. It is impossible that it be contained by books.
The knowledge of books is an indication of the knowledge
of hearts. None contains what the hearts contain except
for the Knower of the Unseen worlds.
Man is helped by books while he does not see the Beloved.
When he sees the Beloved, books are helped by him.

SHAYKH SAYYID MUHAMMAD AS-SANUSI

Shaykh Sayyid Muhammad as-Sanusi, the founder of the Sanusi Order of Algeria, was born into a distinguished family, which was noted for its many learned men who were influential in many localities, near Mustaganim in northern Algeria in about 1787. He was instructed in all the traditional Islamic sciences by a number of teachers at an early age. He learned the entire Qur'an by heart and excelled in his understanding of the recorded actions and sayings of the Prophet Muhammad, the nature of existence, Islamic jurisprudence and the Arabic language. In the company of his teachers, he moved about from place to place, living in such towns as Tlemsen, Mu'askara and Mustaganim, before travelling to Fes where he continued his studies at the Qarawiyyin mosque-university. There he studied all the Qur'anic sciences and the science of Unity, and became so well-versed that he attained great distinction in the spiritual knowledges.

Shaykh as-Sanusi departed from many of the more rigid viewpoints and customs which had been adopted blindly by many religious pseudo-scholars, to the extent that he earned both the hatred of the arrogant scholars for his freedom in interpretation, and the love of many others for his having a piercing intellect, wisdom and perception. Shaykh as-Sanusi always sought to unite all Muslims by following the general consensus of the Muslim community, and by recalling them to the basic path of original Islam, thereby discarding internal strife and dispute.

Shaykh as-Sanusi travelled to Libya in 1853, when he was in his sixties, and designed and commissioned to be built what was shortly to become the great sanctuary-university at Jaghbub. He died six years later in 1859, and was succeeded by his elder son. Following his death, the Sanusi Order created a network of Sufi sanctuaries that extended to every region of the Sahara and beyond its southern fringes. As well as being centres for spiritual activities, these Sufi sanctuaries also provided people with better methods for improving their resources. The social structure of the Sanusi Order ensured a balanced economic and political base as well as a spiritually vibrant society. Under the onslaught of first the French and then the Italian occupation, which was enforced by the use of superior military technology, the members of the Sanusi Order who opposed the colonial forces were considerably depleted in number and their influence was accordingly diminished.

During his lifetime Shaykh Muhammad as-Sanusi succeeded in uniting all the tribes of the region through his teaching and training. He advised people to direct themselves towards Allah, and to submit themselves completely to Him, both in heart and form, so as neither to see, nor hear, nor witness anything else.

SHAYKH MUZAFFER

Shaykh Muzaffer was born in Istanbul in 1916. His father, Hajji Mehmed Efendi of Qonya, was an Islamic scholar and a teacher at the court of Sultan Abdal-Hamid. His mother was the grand-daughter of Shaykh Seyyid Efendi, the spiritual master of the Halveti Order in the town of Yanbolu. On his father's death, when he was only six years old, Muzaffer was taken into the care of Shaykh Seyyid Samiyyi Saruhani of the Qadiri, Naqshbandi, Ushaki and Halveti Orders. From an early age, he studied the Qur'an, the recorded actions and sayings of the Prophet Muhammad and Islamic Law, under the guidance of the spiritual leader of the Fateh mosque in Istanbul and Arnavut Husrev. Hafiz Ismail, the son of the famous musician Zekai Efendi of the Mevlavi Order, taught him many religious hymns and odes. Later on he was appointed as the spiritual leader of the Veznejiler mosque, where he served for 23 years. When that mosque collapsed and was destroyed, he was appointed as the spiritual leader of the mosque in the Covered Bazaar in Istanbul. As well as being the spiritual leader in these two mosques, he also taught and preached to people in 42 other mosques in Istanbul, including the famous Blue Mosque.

Shaykh Muzaffer's first spiritual master was his benefactor Shaykh Samiyyi Saruhani. After him, he encountered another spiritual master of the Halveti Order, Shaykh Seyyid Tahiru'l-Marashi, and several others. He was initiated into the Halveti-Jerrahi Order by Shaykh Fahri Efendi, and later on, he himself became the spiritual master of this order after the death of his master. Despite the attempts of Ataturk and his successors to destroy the Sufis and Islam in Turkey, Shaykh Muzaffer continued to teach until his death in 1986, by which time there were members of his order not only throughout Turkey, but also in Europe, England, North America and elsewhere.

Shaykh Muzaffer's teaching is primarily based on spiritual love and is concerned with the relationship between the lover and the Beloved. In the following verse he says:

> Pass the rest by and follow love, O heart;
> Reality's folk obey love, for their part;
> Love is more ancient than all that's known to exist:
> They sought Love's beginning, but found it had no start.

INDEX